**Grades
4th-Adult**

Learning
the
Continents

C0-BJJ-385

Reproducible
Maps
Activities
Questions

JAMES L. SHOEMAKER
AUTHOR
RANDY L. WOMACK, M.ED.
CO-AUTHOR

™

PUBLISHED BY

G.E.C. PUBLICATIONS

"LEADING THE WAY IN CREATIVE EDUCATIONAL MATERIALS" ™

857 LAKE BLVD. ❖ REDDING, CALIFORNIA 96003
www.goldened.com

TEACHER – PARENT INSTRUCTIONS FOR *Learning the Continents*

Geography is very important! This book was written to be a supplemental resource for social studies and geography programs, as well as a source for introducing children to the world. It is devoted to providing the learners with several intriguing activities that will enable them to learn the countries of the world, the bodies of water and various points of interest.

This book is divided into six sections. The first section is about the world as a whole. The next five sections are each devoted to a major continent. (We had to omit Antarctica and Australia because there was not enough information on these two continents to fit into the book's format.) The activity pattern within each of the five continent sections is identical:

1. Using a completed map, list the countries, bodies of water and points of interest.
2. Fill in a blank map.using the list of countries, bodies of water and points of interest.
3. Review your knowledge of where the countries, bodies of water and points of interest are located.
4. Draw a map and label it correctly.
5. List the bordering countries and waterways of certain countries.
6. Do final review to check your knowledge of where the countries, bodies of water and points of interest are located.
7. Have fun with a word search of the continent's countries, bodies of water and points of interest.

Utilizing this process, students can learn the location of world countries, bodies of water and points of interest. The activities will then make these more relevant to the students when the various parts of the world are discussed, heard about on the news, or become part of their travel plans.

The nature of our world is that it is constantly changing. These maps and activities are accurate as of this printing (August 1994). We realize that countries change their names, boundaries often change and new countries are created and old ones sometimes disintegrate. But this, too, is a lesson in geography.

The maps have been purposely simplified for ease of identification. In accordance with our primary objective of stimulating students to learn the counties of the world, we have made it easier for children to visually discriminate one item at a time, without having unnecessary markings.

We truly hope you and your students will enjoy completing the activities in this book. We also hope that they are used to stimulate further, in-depth studies of the countries of the world.

Thanks a ton!

Jim & Randy

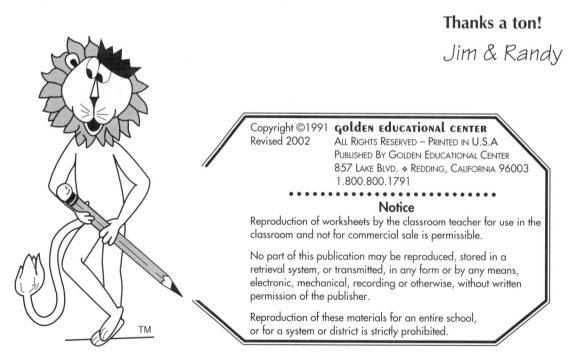

Copyright ©1991 **GOLDEN EDUCATIONAL CENTER**
Revised 2002   ALL RIGHTS RESERVED – PRINTED IN U.S.A
PUBLISHED BY GOLDEN EDUCATIONAL CENTER
857 LAKE BLVD. ❖ REDDING, CALIFORNIA 96003
1.800.800.1791

• • • • • • • • • • • • • • • • • • • •

ISBN 1–56500–018–8

The Continents

❖ **Continental Drift Theory** ❖
❖ **United Nations Information** ❖

This statue — *Let Us Beat Swords Into Plowshares* — stands on the grounds of the United Nations headquarters in New York City.

Continental Drift

Use with page three.

This map shows the land mass scientists call *Pangaea.*

Some people believe this is how the earth looked 200 million years ago. They refer to this land mass as the *'Supercontinent.'*

The map below shows the *Pangaea* land mass broken up into the land masses called *Laurasia* and *Gondwanaland.*

Some people believe this is how the earth looked 65 million years ago. The arrows show the direction in which each of the continents moved.

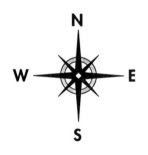

Continental Drift

Use with page two.

Name _____

Date _____

| Find the words in **bold** type in a dictionary and write the meanings on another piece of paper. |

Continental Drift is the name of the **theory** that says the continents were once all connected and have moved great distances on the surface of the earth. This theory also contends that the continents are still moving today. The name scientists have given to the single land **mass** in this theory is *Pangaea*. They believe Pangaea was formed about 200 million years ago.

Today, more than half of the land lies in the Northern Hemisphere. According to this theory, half of Pangaea was in the Southern Hemisphere. What is now the United States was supposed to lie near the Equator, and perhaps farther east of its present location. India, which was then not part of Asia, was supposed to lie near the South Pole.

According to the theory, about 65 million years ago Pangaea began to break up into two large land masses. The northern one was named *Gondwanaland*; and the southern mass was named *Laurasia* by scientists. Gondwanaland and Laurasia began to break up into the present continents and move (drift) towards their present locations. The movement of the land masses was believed to be only about one inch per year, except India might have moved two inches per year.

Some scientists believe, by using the theory of Continental Drift, that the coast of California will break away from the mainland and drift toward Alaska. South America and Africa will move farther apart. Australia will drift north and may collide with Asia.

Alfred Wegener, a German scientist, is considered the father of the Continental Drift Theory. He introduced the theory in 1912 and named Pangaea in 1915.

In the mid-1900's a Scottish **geologist**, Arthur Holmes, **proposed** that hot rock rises from deep within the earth. As it rises and gets closer to the earth's surface, it cools and then sinks back down. Holmes suggested that these circulating movements could cause the continents to move. These circulating movements are called *convection currents*.

Most of today's scientists believe that the continents have moved in the past. However, many of the details of the theory have not been accepted. The biggest problem with the theory is the lack of proof that convection currents exist, and that they provide the force that moves the continents.

Since the 1960's dozens of scientific proofs make the conclusion that the universe is expanding. With this information and other more recent scientific discoveries, scientists can now calculate the origin of the universe to be only 16 billion years ago. **Volumes** of other **data** show that the earth is not more than 20 billion years old — thus making earth much too young for the evolution process to produce anything **akin** to life.[1]

❑ ❑ ❑ ❑ ❑ ❑ ❑ ❑ ❑ ❑ ❑ ❑ ❑ ❑ ❑ ❑

1. Ross, Hugh (1991). *Fingerprint of God* (2nd Edition). Orange, CA: Promise Publishing Company.

© Golden Educational Center

LEARNING THE CONTINENTS: **Continental Drift** – 3

United Nations

Use with page five.

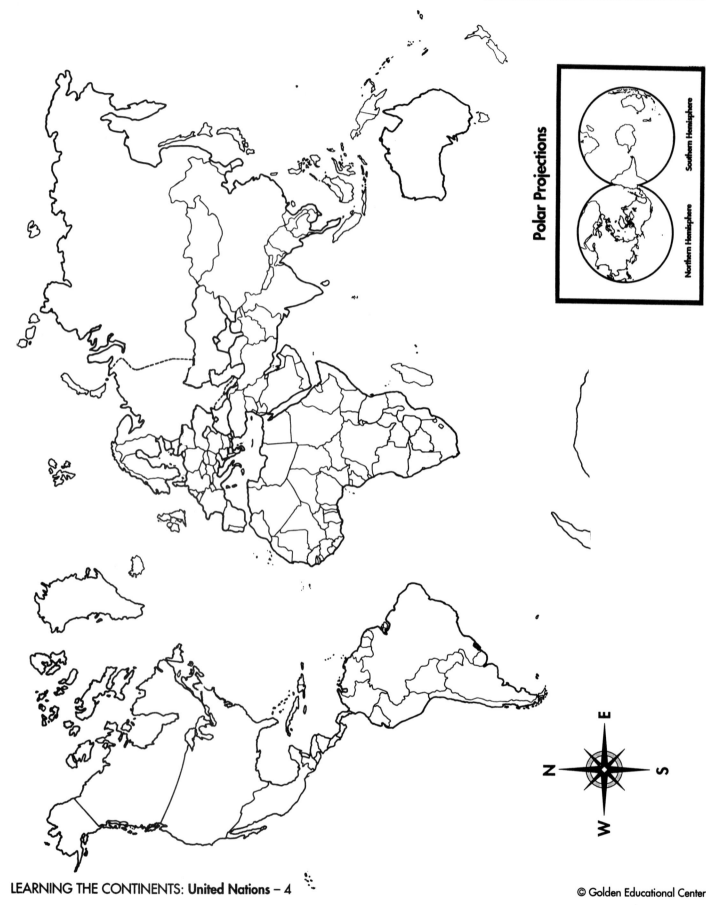

Polar Projections

Northern Hemisphere

Southern Hemisphere

N E W S

United Nations

Use with page five.

Find the words in **bold** type in a dictionary and write the meanings on another piece of paper.

The United Nations was established on October 24, 1945, shortly after World War II. Near the end of World War II, the nations that were fighting against Germany, Italy and Japan never wanted to have such a war happen again. Officials of these nations met in San Francisco, California in April of 1945. They developed a plan for one organization to help keep peace in the world. This plan was called the *Charter of the United Nations*. In June of 1945, fifty nations signed the UN Charter. They were the first (charter) members of the United Nations. Over 100 other countries have joined the organization since the **initial** membership in 1945.

All of the great military powers of the world except Communist China were UN members from the beginning. Communist China gained membership in 1971. In addition to military power to help control and **monitor** worldwide conflicts, the UN is also concerned with **economic** and **social** problems.

There are six organs (branches) of the United Nations that have different responsibilities and perform different tasks. The UN headquarters is located in New York City, along the East River. The flags of all of the member nations fly in front of the UN headquarters.

The Charter (or **Constitution**) of the United Nations includes four purposes of the organization. They are:

1. To preserve world peace and security.
2. To encourage nations to be just in their actions toward each other.
3. To help countries cooperate in trying to solve their problems.
4. To serve as an agency through which nations can work toward these goals.

United Nations – Charter Members

1. Argentina
2. Australia
3. Belgium
4. Bolivia
5. Brazil
6. Canada
7. Chile
8. China (Nationalist)
9. Colombia
10. Costa Rica
11. Cuba
12. Czechoslovakia
13. Denmark
14. Dominican Republic
15. Ecuador
16. Egypt
17. El Salvador
18. Ethiopia
19. France
20. Great Britain
21. Greece
22. Guatemala
23. Haiti
24. Honduras
25. India
26. Iran
27. Iraq
28. Lebanon
29. Liberia
30. Luxembourg
31. Mexico
32. Netherlands
33. New Zealand
34. Nicaragua
35. Norway
36. Panama
37. Paraguay
38. Peru
39. Philippines
40. Poland
41. Russia (U.S.S.R.)
42. Saudi Arabia
43. South Africa
44. Syria
45. Turkey
46. Ukrainian S.S.R
47. United States
48. Uruguay
49. Venezuela
50. Yugoslavia

On the world map provided, find the 50 charter members of the United Nations and mark them somehow, (i.e., color each country in; write the name of each one).

Note: You will probably need to use another resource book for this activity.

NOTES & DOODLES

NOTES & DOODLES

Africa
Country Identification

Africa
Use with page nine.

Name _____

Date _____

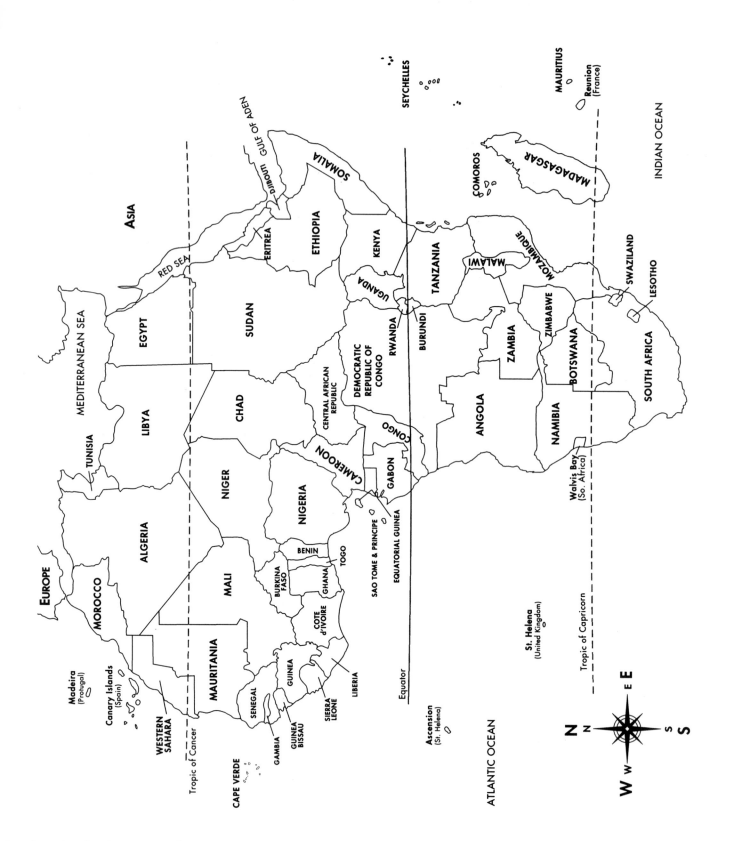

Learning the Continents: **Africa** – 8

© Golden Educational Center

Africa

Use with page eight.

Name _____

Date _____

Label this map exactly like the map provided. Make sure you print the names the same.

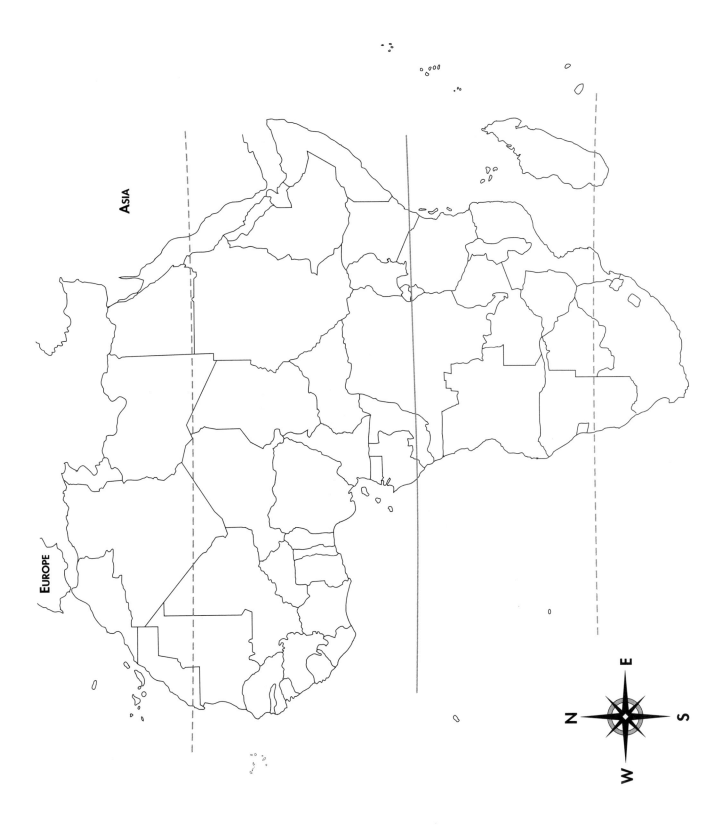

Africa

Use with page eleven.

Name _____

Date _____

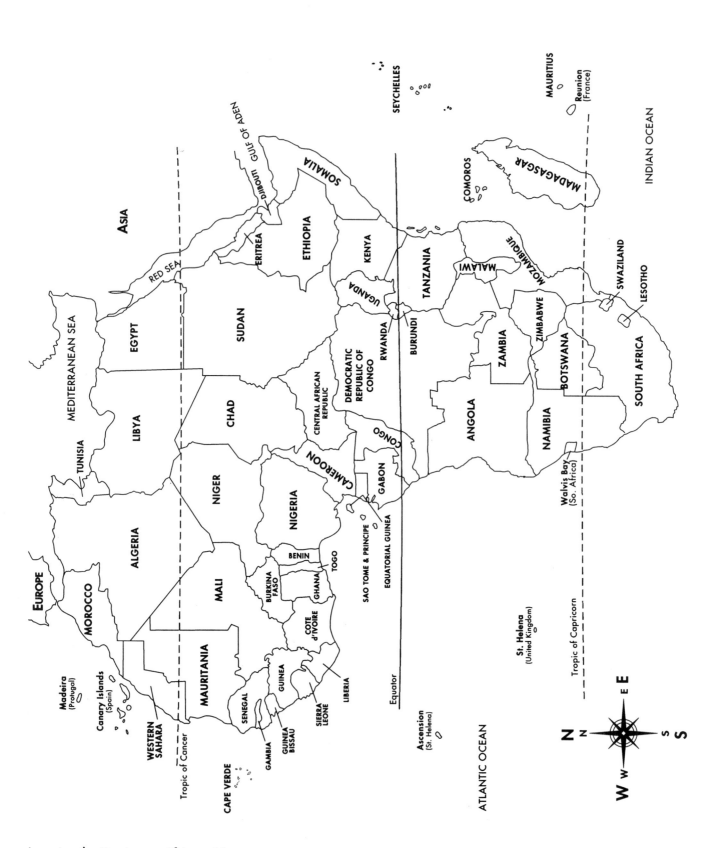

**Africa**

Use with page ten.

Name _____

Date _____

Fill in the lines with the correct answer in alphabetical order using the map provided.
Note the style of type when choosing the words for the appropriate line.

INDEPENDENT COUNTRIES   MAJOR WATERWAYS   **Other Political Units**   Points of Interest

INDEPENDENT COUNTRIES

1. _____
2. _____
3. _____
4. _____
5. _____
6. _____
7. _____
8. _____
9. _____
10. _____
11. _____
12. _____
13. _____
14. _____
15. _____
16. _____
17. _____
18. _____
19. _____
20. _____
21. _____
22. _____
23. _____
24. _____
25. _____
26. _____
27. _____
28. _____
29. _____
30. _____
31. _____
32. _____
33. _____
34. _____
35. _____

INDEPENDENT COUNTRIES

36. _____
37. _____
38. _____
39. _____
40. _____
41. _____
42. _____
43. _____
44. _____
45. _____
46. _____
47. _____
48. _____
49. _____
50. _____
51. _____
52. _____
53. _____

❖ Waterways ❖ Points of Interest ❖
❖ Other Political Units ❖

_____
_____
_____
_____
_____
_____
_____
_____
_____
_____
_____

Africa

Use with page thirteen.

Name _____

Date _____

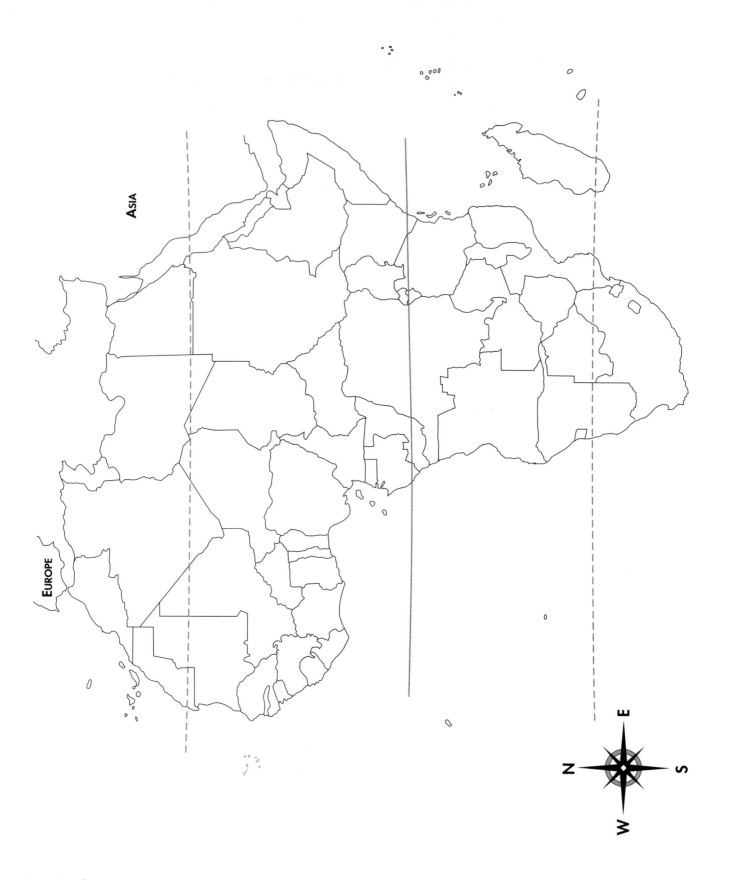

ASIA

EUROPE

N E S W

Fill in the map provided with the correct country, waterway or point of interest.
Note the style of type when choosing the words for the appropriate label.

INDEPENDENT COUNTRIES   MAJOR WATERWAYS   **Other Political Units**   Points of Interest

INDEPENDENT COUNTRIES

1. **ALGERIA**
2. **ANGOLA**
3. **BENIN**
4. **BOTSWANA**
5. **BURKINA FASO**
6. **BURUNDI**
7. **CAMEROON**
8. **CAPE VERDE**
9. **CENTRAL AFRICAN REPUBLIC**
10. **CHAD**
11. **COMOROS**
12. **CONGO**
13. **COTE D'IVOIRE** (Ivory Coast)
14. **DEMOCRATIC REP. OF CONGO** (Zaire)
15. **DJIBOUTI**
16. **EGYPT**
17. **EQUATORIAL GUINEA**
18. **ERITREA**
19. **ETHIOPIA**
20. **GABON**
21. **GAMBIA**
22. **GHANA**
23. **GUINEA**
24. **GUINEA-BISSAU**
25. **KENYA**
26. **LESOTHO**
27. **LIBERIA**
28. **LIBYA**
29. **MADAGASCAR**
30. **MALAWI**
31. **MALI**
32. **MAURITANIA**
33. **MAURITIUS**
34. **MOROCCO**
35. **MOZAMBIQUE**

INDEPENDENT COUNTRIES

36. **NAMIBIA** (South West Africa)
37. **NIGER**
38. **NIGERIA**
39. **RWANDA**
40. **SÃO TOMÉ and PRINCIPE**
41. **SENEGAL**
42. **SEYCHELLES**
43. **SIERRA LEONE**
44. **SOMALIA**
45. **SOUTH AFRICA**
46. **SUDAN**
47. **SWAZILAND**
48. **TANZANIA**
49. **TOGO**
50. **TUNISIA**
51. **UGANDA**
52. **ZAMBIA**
53. **ZIMBABWE**

❖ WATERWAYS ❖ POINTS OF INTEREST ❖
❖ OTHER POLITICAL UNITS ❖

ATLANTIC OCEAN
EQUATOR
CANARY ISLANDS (Spain)
GULF OF ADEN
INDIAN OCEAN
MADEIRA ISLANDS (Portugal)
MEDITERRANEAN SEA
RED SEA
REUNION (France)
ST. HELENA (United Kingdom)
TROPIC OF CANCER
TROPIC OF CAPRICORN
WALVIS BAY (South Africa)
WESTERN SAHARA (Occupied by Morocco)

Africa: Review #1
Use with page fifteen.

Name _____

Date _____

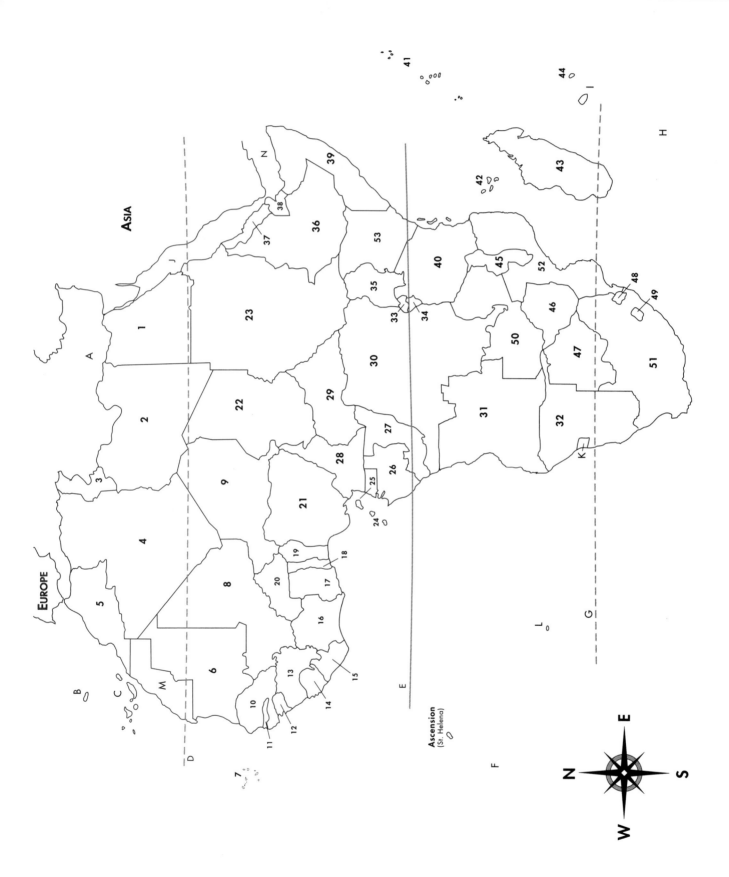

Ascension
(St. Helena)

Africa: Review #1

Use with page fourteen.

Name _____

Date _____

Fill in the lines with the correct number or letter using the map provided.
Note: "O" was not used because it could be mistaken for an island on the map.

INDEPENDENT COUNTRIES

_____ ALGERIA
_____ ANGOLA
_____ BENIN
_____ BOTSWANA
_____ BURKINA FASO
_____ BURUNDI
_____ CAMEROON
_____ CAPE VERDE
_____ CENTRAL AFRICAN REPUBLIC
_____ CHAD
_____ COMOROS
_____ CONGO
_____ DEMOCRATIC REPUBLIC OF CONGO
_____ COTE D'IVOIRE (Ivory Coast)
_____ DJIBOUTI
_____ EGYPT
_____ EQUATORIAL GUINEA
_____ ERITREA
_____ ETHIOPIA
_____ GABON
_____ GAMBIA
_____ GHANA
_____ GUINEA
_____ GUINEA-BISSAU
_____ KENYA
_____ LESOTHO
_____ LIBERIA
_____ LIBYA
_____ MADAGASCAR
_____ MALAWI
_____ MALI
_____ MAURITANIA
_____ MAURITIUS
_____ MOROCCO
_____ MOZAMBIQUE

INDEPENDENT COUNTRIES

_____ NAMIBIA (South West Africa)
_____ NIGER
_____ NIGERIA
_____ RWANDA
_____ SÃO TOMÉ and PRINCIPE
_____ SENEGAL
_____ SEYCHELLES
_____ SIERRA LEONE
_____ SOMALIA
_____ SOUTH AFRICA
_____ SUDAN
_____ SWAZILAND
_____ TANZANIA
_____ TOGO
_____ TUNISIA
_____ UGANDA
_____ ZAMBIA
_____ ZIMBABWE

❖ WATERWAYS ❖ POINTS OF INTEREST ❖ ❖ OTHER POLITICAL UNITS ❖

_____ ATLANTIC OCEAN
_____ EQUATOR
_____ CANARY ISLANDS (Spain)
_____ GULF OF ADEN
_____ INDIAN OCEAN
_____ MADEIRA ISLANDS (Portugal)
_____ MEDITERRANEAN SEA
_____ RED SEA
_____ REUNION (France)
_____ ST. HELENA (United Kingdom)
_____ TROPIC OF CANCER
_____ TROPIC OF CAPRICORN
_____ WALVIS BAY (South Africa)
_____ WESTERN SAHARA (Occupied by Morocco)

Africa

Use with page seventeen.

Name _____

Date _____

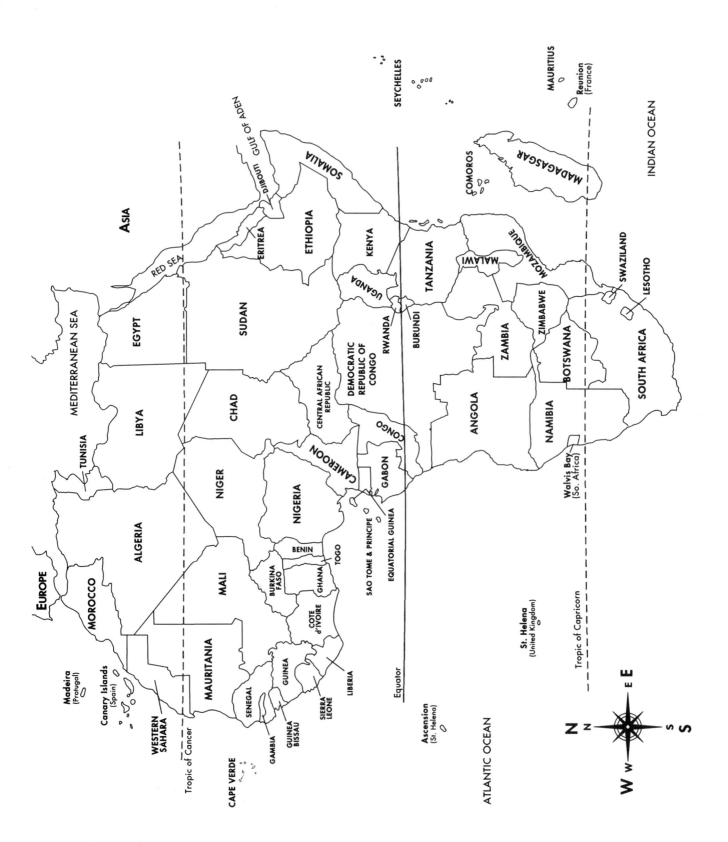

Africa

Use with page sixteen.

Name _____

Date _____

Trace the outline of Africa and then draw in the countries, etc. Label your map.

Africa

Use with page nineteen.

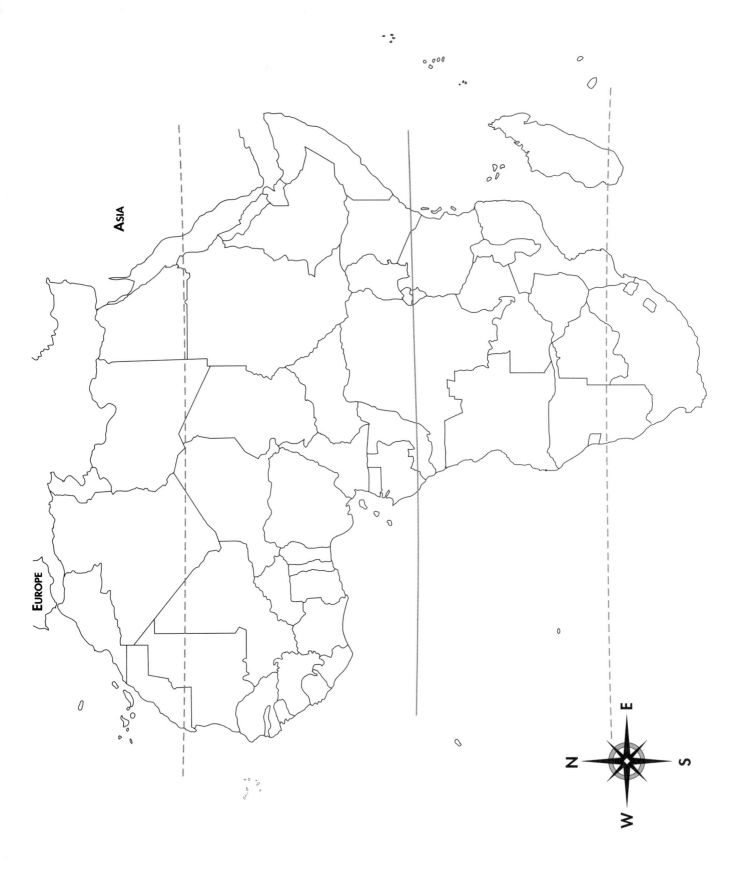

Africa

Name _____

Date _____

Fill in the lines with the correct bordering countries and/or waterways using the map provided. The number following the name of each country specifies the number of names you need to write. Note: You might need to complete the map before you begin.

ALGERIA (8) _____

_____

ANGOLA (4) _____

BENIN (5) _____

_____

BOTSWANA (3) _____

BURUNDI (3) _____

CAMEROON (7) _____

_____

CHAD (6) _____

_____

CONGO (5) _____

_____

COTE D'IVOIRE (6) _____

_____

DJIBOUTI (4) _____

EGYPT (4) _____

ETHIOPIA (5) _____

_____

GAMBIA (2) _____

_____

KENYA (6) _____

_____

MADAGASCAR (1) _____

NIGER (7) _____

_____

NIGERIA (5) _____

_____

SOMALIA (4) _____

_____

SOUTH AFRICA (8) _____

_____

UGANDA (5) _____

_____

Africa: Review #2

Use with page twenty-one.

Name _____

Date _____

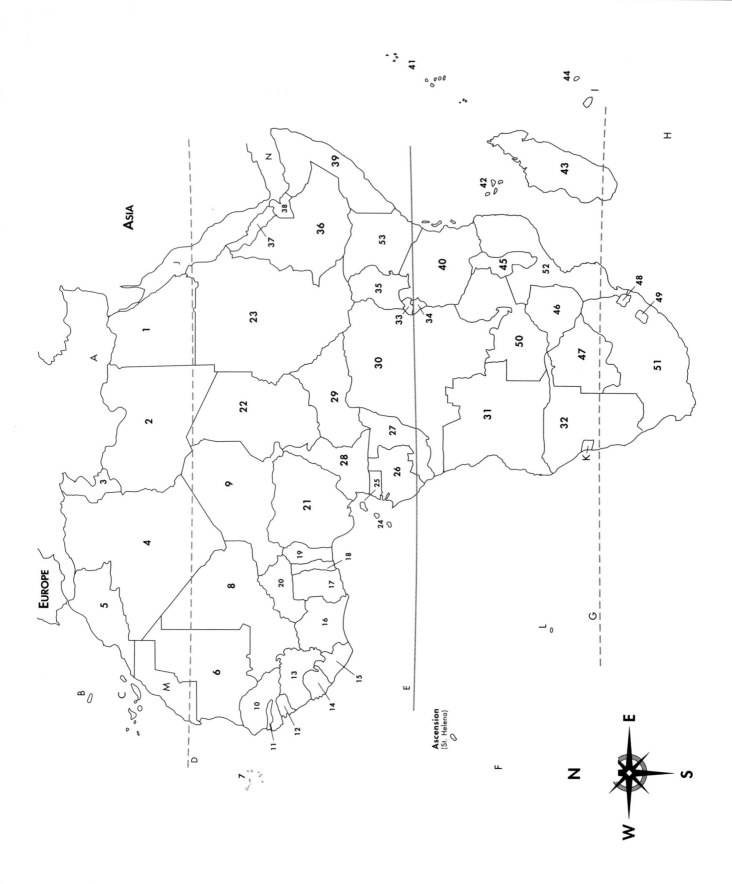

Africa: Review #2

Use with page twenty.

Name _____

Date _____

Write the name of the correct answer next to the corresponding number
or letter on the line provided.

INDEPENDENT COUNTRIES

1. _____
2. _____
3. _____
4. _____
5. _____
6. _____
7. _____
8. _____
9. _____
10. _____
11. _____
12. _____
13. _____
14. _____
15. _____
16. _____
17. _____
18. _____
19. _____
20. _____
21. _____
22. _____
23. _____
24. _____
25. _____
26. _____
27. _____
28. _____
29. _____
30. _____
31. _____
32. _____
33. _____
34. _____
35. _____

INDEPENDENT COUNTRIES

36. _____
37. _____
38. _____
39. _____
40. _____
41. _____
42. _____
43. _____
44. _____
45. _____
46. _____
47. _____
48. _____
49. _____
50. _____
51. _____
52. _____
53. _____

❖ Waterways ❖ Points of Interest ❖
❖ Other Political Units ❖

A. _____
B. _____
C. _____
D. _____
E. _____
F. _____
G. _____
H. _____
I. _____
J. _____
K. _____
L. _____
M. _____
N. _____

Africa
Word Search
(No space between words.)

ALGERIA	IVORY COAST	RWANDA
ANGOLA	KENYA	SOMALIA
CONGO	LESOTHO	SOUTH AFRICA
DJIBOUTI	LIBERIA	SUDAN
EGYPT	LIBYA	SWAZILAND
GAMBIA	MADAGASCAR	TANZANIA
GHANA	NAMIBIA	UGANDA
GUINEA	NIGERIA	ZIMBABWE

```
L A T S F K A G R C H Z N O R C T P Y T V
U I L A P M D N U W X K U J H D T L H Q R
G V B G N K A H G I A X L U H Q D V B N D
A W M E E Z D D X O N N J E W S J D E M Z
N S J E R R A N A A L E D O S I A L P P Y
D P A G L I I N A G I A A A P G O Q C K P
A X U Y D K A A I L A R D Z C Z M Y Y E U
K Y J P E E C L P A I S E G J P Q P I O N
B S X T U N X J V L V Z C G V J S L J J I
M L E P A Y O S U A U J A A I X I I T Z R
B G K P S A D A A S T O I W R N T A I K N
C V A V U N T S H A Y B I L S U C M E A S
S U D A N P V R N C N C X P O I B O M E D
Q V L J L M B Q M E B Y T B R A H I N Z G
M A F Q Y S Q T G Z Y P I F B T B E A P F
M A V L A I E K S F O J A W O I G I I I E
N I O W A T W P A O D H E S A A B W Y A W
X B G E N U K S J J T Y E G L M A U U D C
P M N I A W Y T S U S L C E A L M L K D A
U A O P H X S F O N T J P G A A K H S S P
T Z C K G Q X S M V U V O M P P H P C M Y
```

Asia
Country Identification

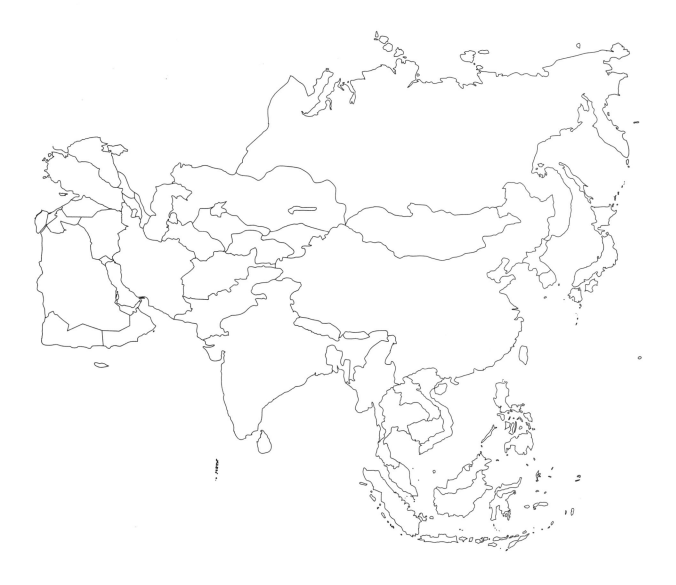

Asia

Use with page twenty-five.

Name _____

Date _____

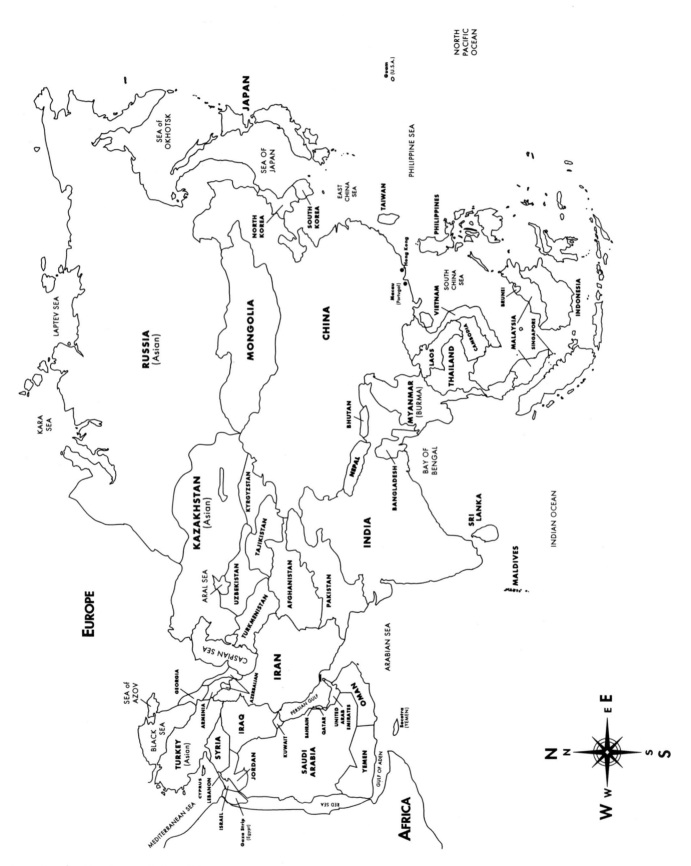

Asia

Use with page twenty-four.

Name _____

Date _____

Label this map exactly like the map provided. Make sure you print the names the same.

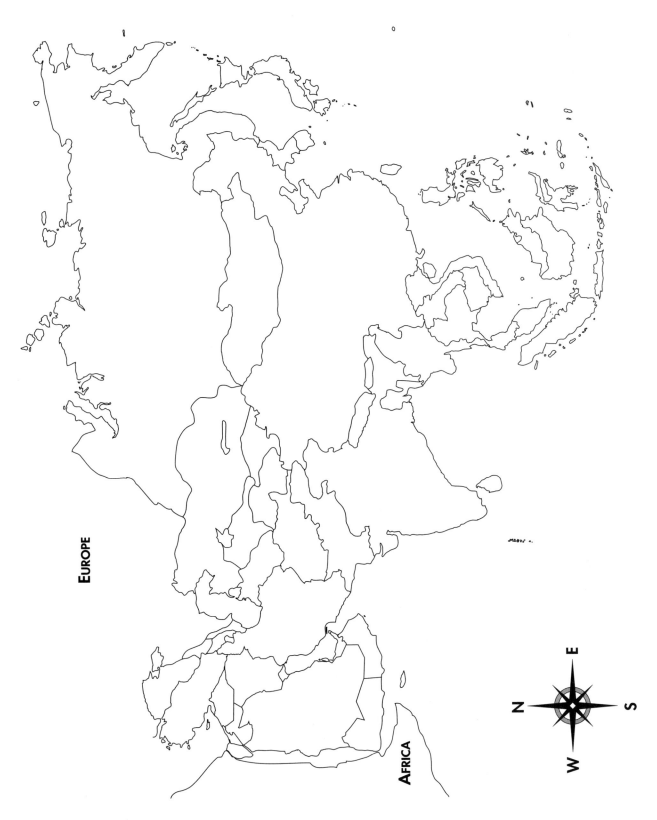

EUROPE

AFRICA

N E S W

Asia

Use with page twenty-seven.

Name _____

Date _____

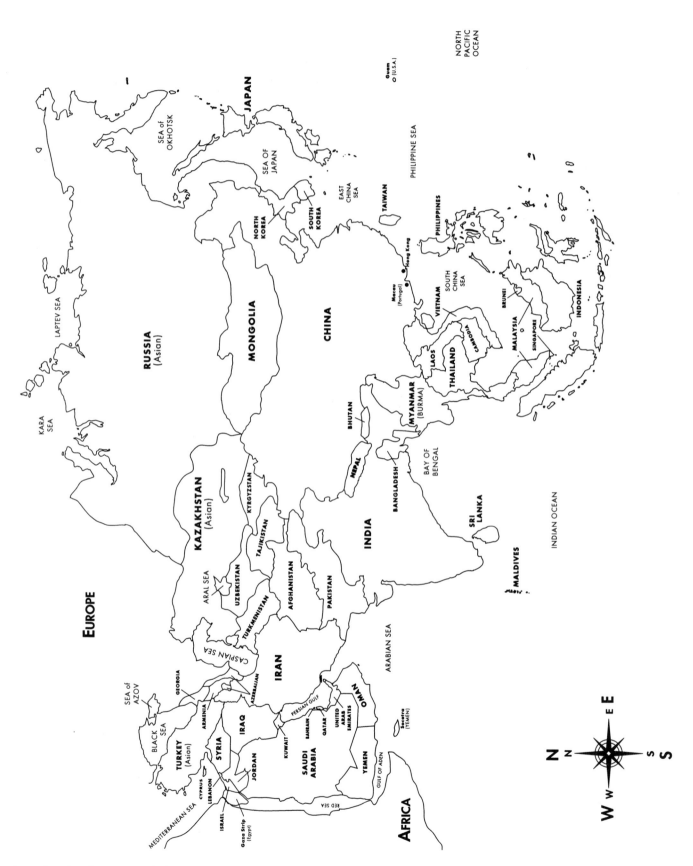

Asia

Use with page twenty-six.

Name _____

Date _____

Fill in the lines with the correct answer in alphabetical order using the map provided.
Note the style of type when choosing the words for the appropriate line.

INDEPENDENT COUNTRIES   MAJOR WATERWAYS   **Other Political Units**   Points of Interest

INDEPENDENT COUNTRIES

1. _____
2. _____
3. _____
4. _____
5. _____
6. _____
7. _____
8. _____
9. _____
10. _____
11. _____
12. _____
13. _____
14. _____
15. _____
16. _____
17. _____
18. _____
19. _____
20. _____
21. _____
22. _____
23. _____
24. _____
25. _____
26. _____
27. _____
28. _____
29. _____
30. _____
31. _____
32. _____
33. _____
34. _____
35. _____
36. _____
37. _____

INDEPENDENT COUNTRIES

38. _____
39. _____
40. _____
41. _____
42. _____
43. _____
44. _____
45. _____
46. _____
47. _____
48. _____

❖ Other Political Units ❖

_____
_____
_____
_____

❖ Major Waterways ❖

_____
_____
_____
_____
_____
_____
_____
_____
_____
_____
_____
_____
_____
_____
_____

Asia

Use with page twenty-nine.

Name _____

Date _____

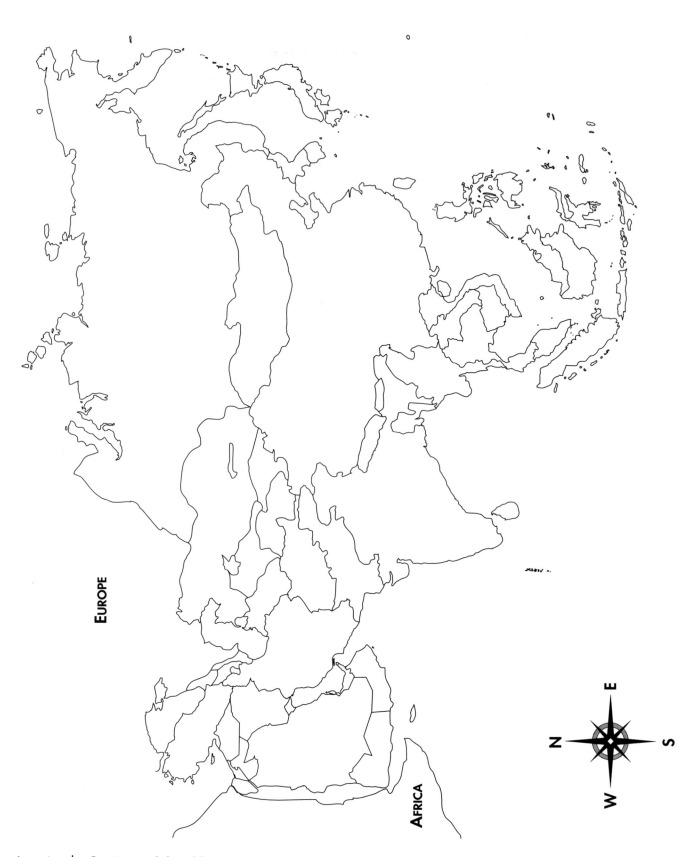

Name _____

Date _____

Fill in the map provided with the correct country, waterway or point of interest.
Note the style of type when choosing the words for the appropriate label.

INDEPENDENT COUNTRIES   MAJOR WATERWAYS   **Other Political Units**   Points of Interest

INDEPENDENT COUNTRIES

1. AFGHANISTAN
2. ARMENIA
3. AZERBAIJAN
4. BAHRAIN
5. BANGLADESH
6. BHUTAN
7. BRUNEI
8. CAMBODIA (also called Kampuchea)
9. CHINA
10. CYPRUS
11. GEORGIA
12. INDIA
13. INDONESIA
14. IRAN
15. IRAQ
16. ISRAEL
17. JAPAN
18. JORDAN
19. KAZAKHSTAN
20. KOREA, NORTH
21. KOREA, SOUTH
22. KUWAIT
23. KYRGYZSTAN
24. LAOS
25. LEBANON
26. MALAYSIA
27. MALDIVES
28. MONGOLIA
29. MYANMAR (also called Burma)
30. NEPAL
31. OMAN
32. PAKISTAN
33. PHILIPPINES
34. QATAR
35. RUSSIA (in Asia)
36. SAUDI ARABIA
37. SINGAPORE

INDEPENDENT COUNTRIES

38. SRI LANKA
39. SYRIA
40. TAIWAN
41. TAJIKISTAN
42. THAILAND
43. TURKEY (in Asia)
44. TURKMENISTAN
45. UNITED ARAB EMIRATES
46. UZBEKISTAN
47. VIETNAM
48. YEMEN

❖ OTHER POLITICAL UNITS ❖

Gaza Strip (Egypt)
Guam (United States)
Hong Kong
Macau

❖ MAJOR WATERWAYS ❖

ARABIAN SEA
ARAL SEA
BLACK SEA
BAY OF BENGAL
CASPIAN SEA
EAST CHINA SEA
GULF OF ADEN
INDIAN OCEAN
KARA SEA
LAPTEV SEA
MEDITERRANEAN SEA
NORTH PACIFIC OCEAN
PERSIAN GULF
PHILIPPINE SEA
RED SEA
SEA OF AZOV
SEA OF JAPAN
SEA OF OKHOTSK
SOUTH CHINA SEA

Asia: Review #1

Use with page thirty-one.

Name _____

Date _____

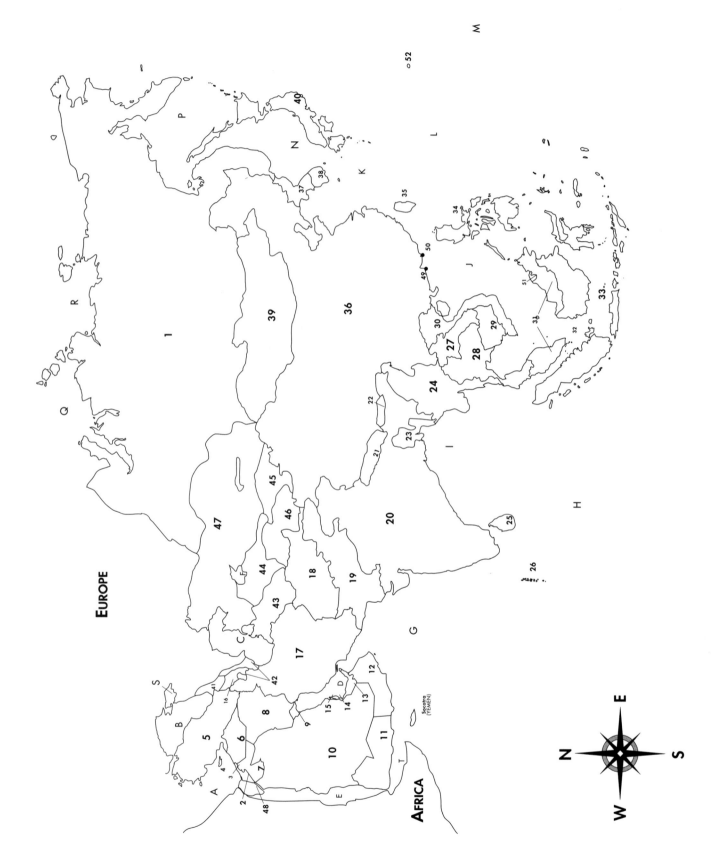

Use with page thirty.

Name _____

Date _____

Fill in the lines with the correct number or letter using the map provided.
Note: "O" was not used because it could be mistaken for an island on the map.

INDEPENDENT COUNTRIES

_____ AFGHANISTAN
_____ ARMENIA
_____ AZERBAIJAN
_____ BAHRAIN
_____ BANGLADESH
_____ BHUTAN
_____ BRUNEI
_____ CAMBODIA (also called Kampuchea)
_____ CHINA
_____ CYPRUS
_____ GEORGIA
_____ INDIA
_____ INDONESIA
_____ IRAN
_____ IRAQ
_____ ISRAEL
_____ JAPAN
_____ JORDAN
_____ KAZAKHSTAN
_____ KOREA, NORTH
_____ KOREA, SOUTH
_____ KUWAIT
_____ KYRGYZSTAN
_____ LAOS
_____ LEBANON
_____ MALAYSIA
_____ MALDIVES
_____ MONGOLIA
_____ MYANMAR (also called Burma)
_____ NEPAL
_____ OMAN
_____ PAKISTAN
_____ PHILIPPINES
_____ QATAR
_____ RUSSIA (in Asia)
_____ SAUDI ARABIA
_____ SINGAPORE

INDEPENDENT COUNTRIES

_____ SRI LANKA
_____ SYRIA
_____ TAIWAN
_____ TAJIKISTAN
_____ THAILAND
_____ TURKEY (in Asia)
_____ TURKMENISTAN
_____ UNITED ARAB EMIRATES
_____ UZBEKISTAN
_____ VIETNAM
_____ YEMEN

❖ OTHER POLITICAL UNITS ❖
_____ Gaza Strip (Egypt)
_____ Guam (United States)
_____ Hong Kong
_____ Macau

❖ MAJOR WATERWAYS ❖
_____ ARABIAN SEA
_____ ARAL SEA
_____ BLACK SEA
_____ BAY OF BENGAL
_____ CASPIAN SEA
_____ EAST CHINA SEA
_____ GULF OF ADEN
_____ INDIAN OCEAN
_____ KARA SEA
_____ LAPTEV SEA
_____ MEDITERRANEAN SEA
_____ NORTH PACIFIC OCEAN
_____ PERSIAN GULF
_____ PHILIPPINE SEA
_____ RED SEA
_____ SEA OF AZOV
_____ SEA OF JAPAN
_____ SEA OF OKHOTSK
_____ SOUTH CHINA SEA

Asia

Name _____

Date _____

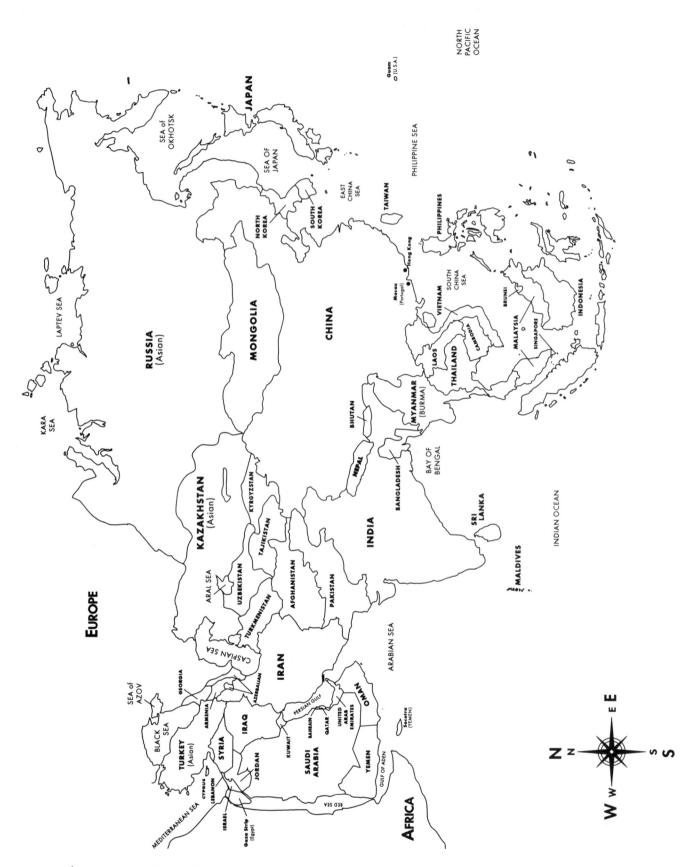

Asia

Use with page thirty-two.

Name _____

Date _____

Trace the outline of Asia and then draw in the countries, etc. Label your map.

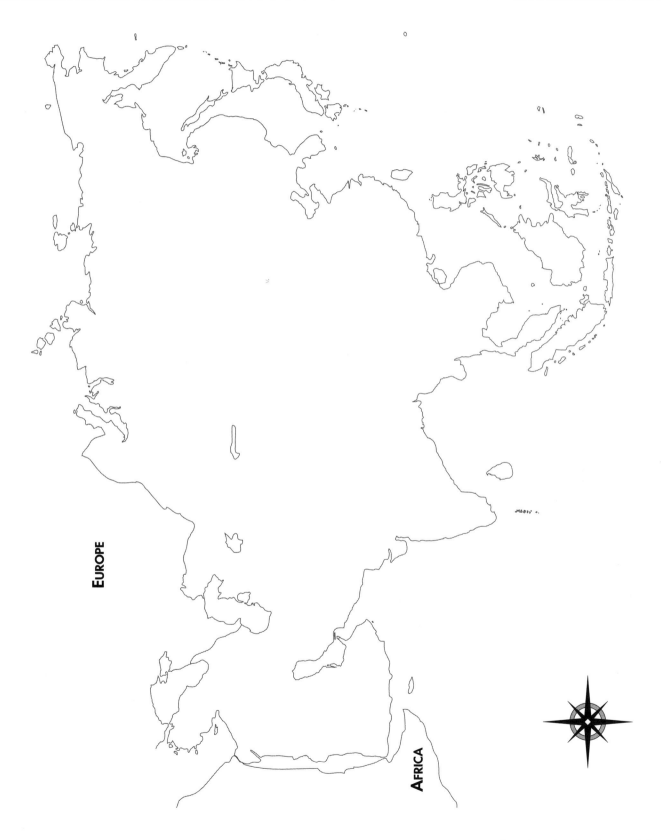

EUROPE

AFRICA

Asia
Use with page thirty-five.

Name _____

Date _____

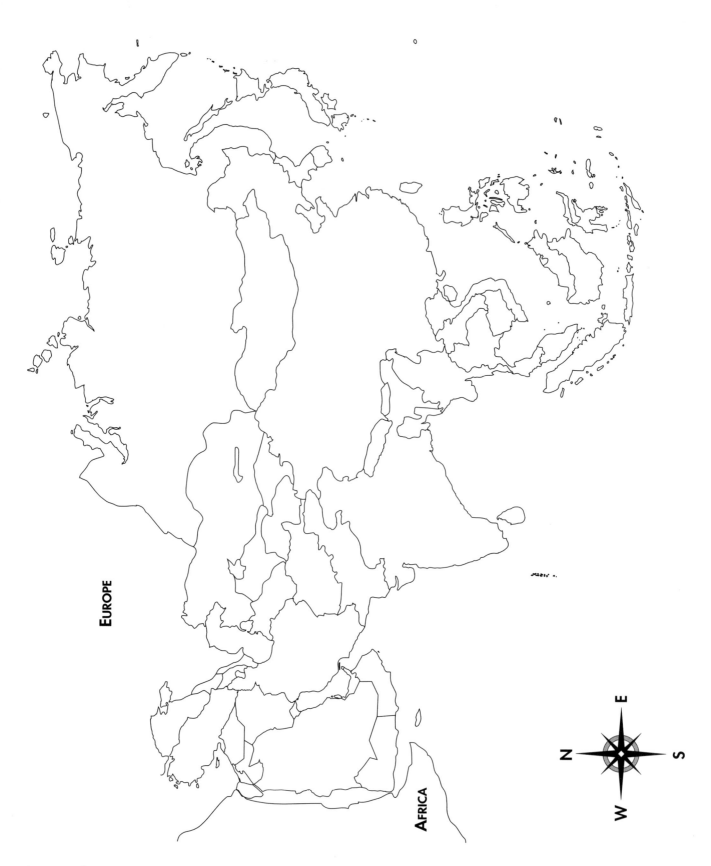

EUROPE

AFRICA

N E S W

Asia

Use with page thirty-six.

Name _____

Date _____

Fill in the lines with the correct bordering countries and/or waterways using the map provided. The number following the name of each country specifies the number of names you need to write. Note: You might need to complete the map before you begin.

AFGHANISTAN (6) _____
_____

BANGLADESH (3) _____
BHUTAN (2) _____
CHINA (15) _____
_____
_____
_____

INDIA (8) _____
_____

IRAN (10) _____
_____
_____

IRAQ (7) _____
_____

ISRAEL (6) _____
JAPAN (3) _____
KAMPUCHEA (4) _____
LEBANON (3) _____
MONGOLIA (2) _____
NEPAL (2) _____
PAKISTAN (5) _____
_____

RUSSIA (10) _____
_____
_____

SAUDI ARABIA (9) _____
_____
_____

TAIWAN (3) _____
THAILAND (5) _____
_____

VIETNAM (5) _____
_____

Name _____

Date _____

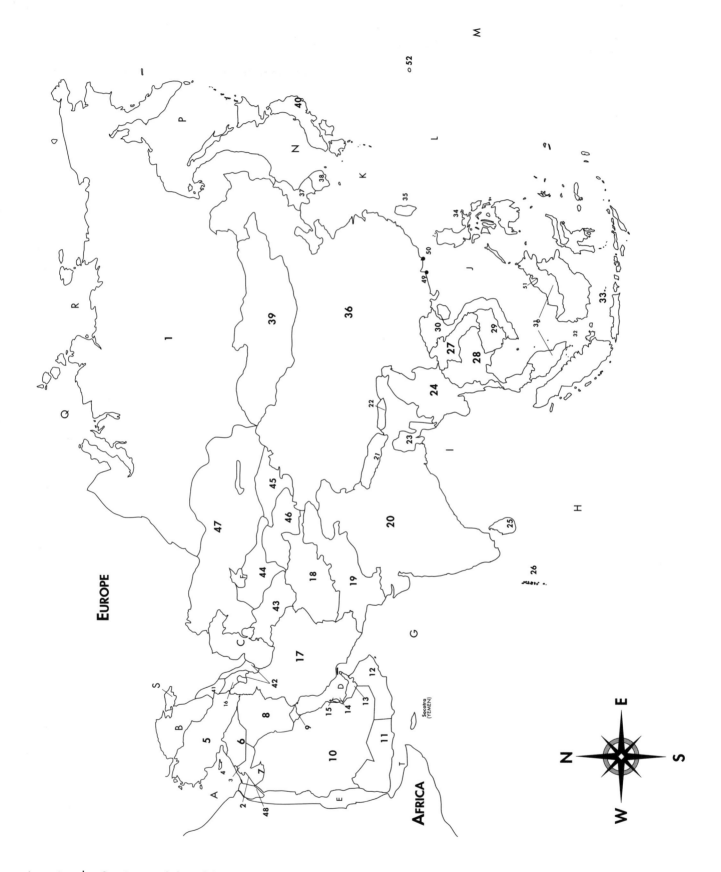

EUROPE

AFRICA

Socotra
(YEMEN)

N
W — E
S

Name _____

Date _____

Write the name of the correct answer next to the corresponding number
or letter on the line provided.

INDEPENDENT COUNTRIES

1. _____
2. _____
3. _____
4. _____
5. _____
6. _____
7. _____
8. _____
9. _____
10. _____
11. _____
12. _____
13. _____
14. _____
15. _____
16. _____
17. _____
18. _____
19. _____
20. _____
21. _____
22. _____
23. _____
24. _____
25. _____
26. _____
27. _____
28. _____
29. _____
30. _____
31. _____
32. _____
33. _____
34. _____
35. _____
36. _____
37. _____

INDEPENDENT COUNTRIES

38. _____
39. _____
40. _____
41. _____
42. _____
43. _____
44. _____
45. _____
46. _____
47. _____
48. _____

❖ Other Political Units ❖

49. _____
50. _____
51. _____
52. _____

❖ MAJOR WATERWAYS ❖

A. _____
B. _____
C. _____
D. _____
E. _____
F. _____
G. _____
H. _____
I. _____
J. _____
K. _____
L. _____
M. _____
N. _____
P. _____
Q. _____
R. _____
S. _____
T. _____

Asia
Word Search
(No space between words.)

Name _____

Date _____

BANGLADESH	JAPAN	SAUDI ARABIA
BURMA	JORDAN	SRI LANKA
CHINA	MALDIVES	SYRIA
CYPRUS	MONGOLIA	TAIWAN
HONG KONG	NORTH KOREA	THAILAND
INDIAN OCEAN	PACIFIC OCEAN	UZBEKISTAN
INDONESIA	PAKISTAN	VIETNAM
ISRAEL	PHILIPPINES	YEMEN

```
J G B J T F M I P Q U G F Y Q F D G M J J
Y I A A A H I A N A R L Z K R D U C U L L
X J N N M P A N L D C O Q H Q P Y C N O T
K L G O V R A I A D O I J L S P O F B O C
C E L R V R U N L T I N F C M H V P L Q B
M M A T R M Y B S A S V E I C K Z W W D I
J I D H Y T E O N U N I E S C X F P G N R
A W E K Y E M G O A R D K S I O W Y D A Q
D R S O C T E V U J D P B A Q A C I S A D
S V H R S E N Y W X I R Y L P Q A E I H M
S A I E A Q I S G S K U O C K N H L A P N
E I E A N U P M V O V A O J O O O B U N D
N B G C A E F A V W G B S C N G Q L I K X
I A S H T B M H V K Y F E G N A V S T R B
P R W P S F Y K C K Z A K O K I R A E Z T
P A G I I V S D H W N O M N E A I S X D Q
I I R Y K A M L V E N C A T E W Y E T S M
L D P J E I Y Q K G H L N L A B S M A J T
I U Y X B R K X S I I A R N Q V K G S O Y
H A E P Z Y J O N R M V B A R Q M Z I E L
P S E I U S W A S K D K X I L V S Q T C B
```

© Golden Educational Center

Europe
Country Identification

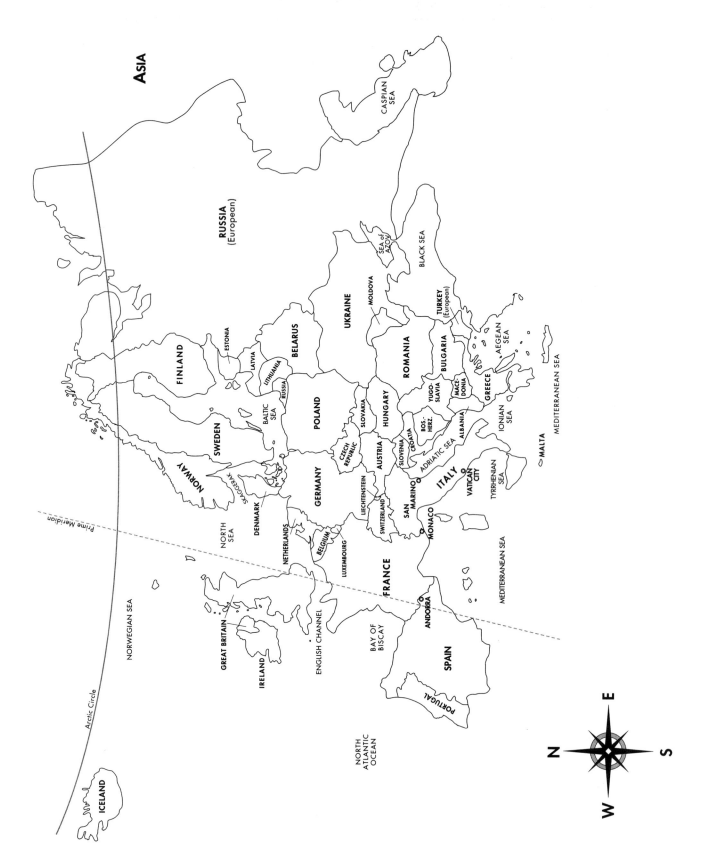

Europe

Use with page forty.

Name _____

Date _____

Label this map exactly like the map provided. Make sure you print the names the same.

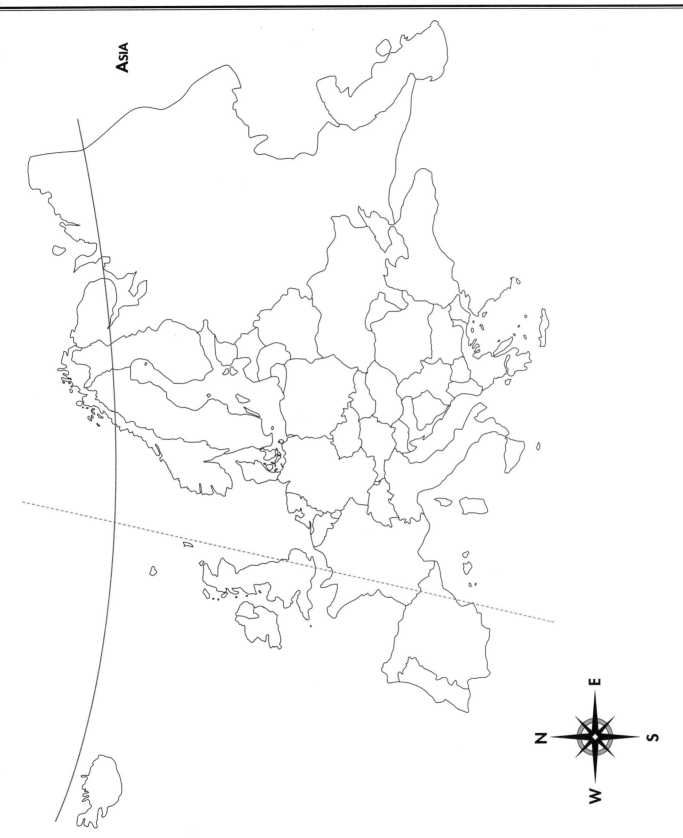

ASIA

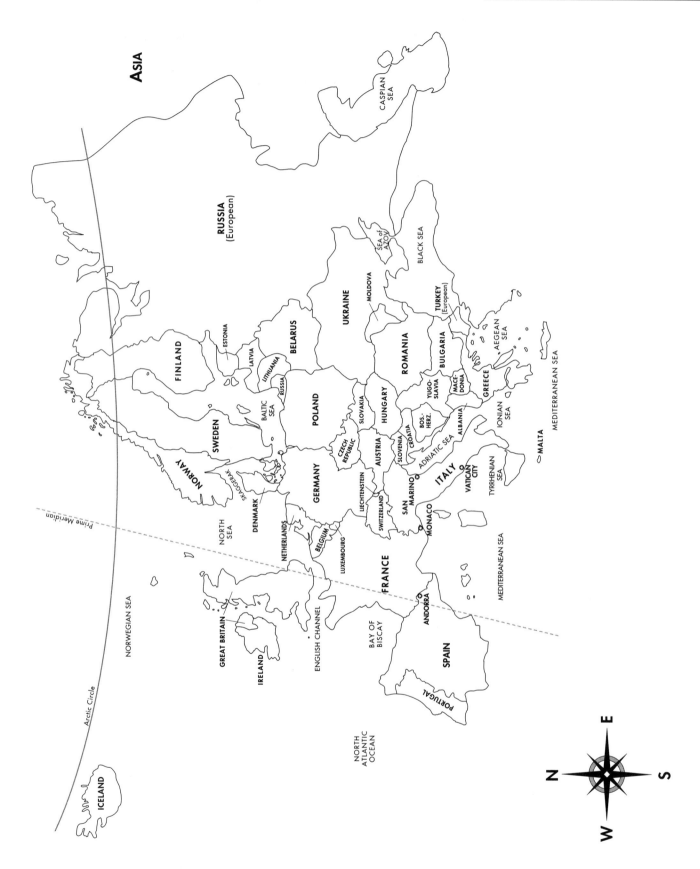

Europe

Use with page forty-two.

Fill in the lines with the correct answer in alphabetical order using the map provided.
Note the style of type when choosing the words for the appropriate line.

INDEPENDENT COUNTRIES   MAJOR WATERWAYS   **Other Political Units**   Points of Interest

INDEPENDENT COUNTRIES

1. _____
2. _____
3. _____
4. _____
5. _____
6. _____
7. _____
8. _____
9. _____
10. _____
11. _____
12. _____
13. _____
14. _____
15. _____
16. _____
17. _____
18. _____
19. _____
20. _____
21. _____
22. _____
23. _____
24. _____
25. _____
26. _____
27. _____
28. _____
29. _____
30. _____
31. _____
32. _____
33. _____
34. _____
35. _____

INDEPENDENT COUNTRIES

36. _____
37. _____
38. _____
39. _____
40. _____
41. _____
42. _____
43. _____
44. _____

❖ WATERWAYS ❖ POINTS OF INTEREST ❖ ❖ OTHER POLITICAL UNITS ❖

_____
_____
_____
_____
_____
_____
_____
_____
_____
_____
_____
_____
_____
_____
_____
_____

Which three countries are located partly in Europe and partly in Asia?

_____
_____
_____

Europe

Use with page forty-five.

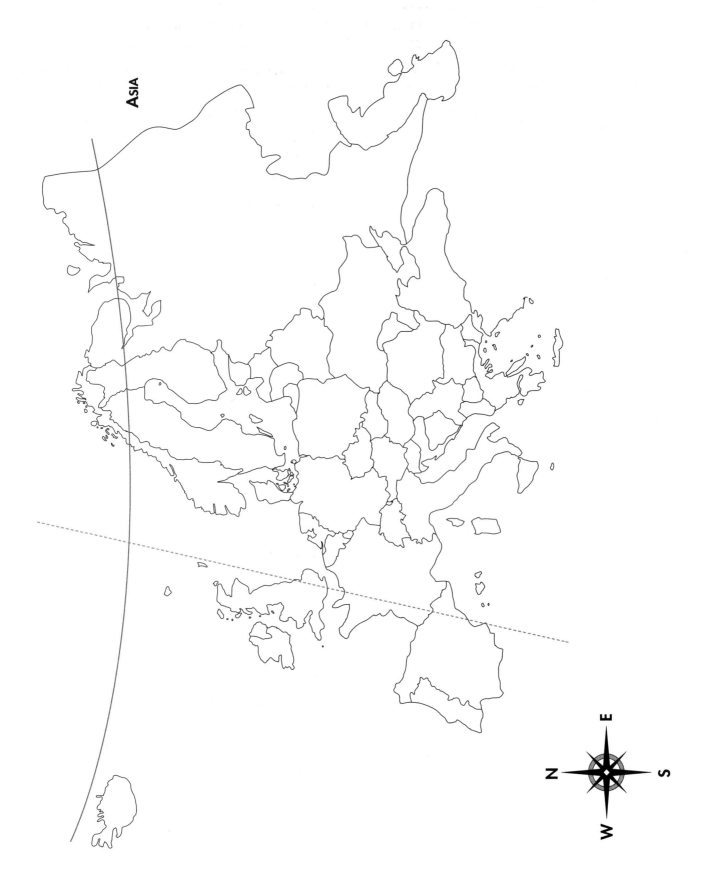

ASIA

Europe

Use with page forty-four.

Name _____

Date _____

Fill in the map provided with the correct country, waterway or point of interest.
Note the style of type when choosing the words for the appropriate label.

INDEPENDENT COUNTRIES   MAJOR WATERWAYS   **Other Political Units**   Points of Interest

INDEPENDENT COUNTRIES

1. **ALBANIA**
2. **ANDORRA** (only a city)
3. **AUSTRIA**
4. **BELARUS**
5. **BELGIUM**
6. **BOSNIA-HERZEGOVINA**
7. **BULGARIA**
8. **CROATIA**
9. **CZECH REPUBLIC**
10. **DENMARK**
11. **ESTONIA**
12. **FINLAND**
13. **FRANCE**
14. **GERMANY**
15. **GREECE**
16. **HUNGARY**
17. **ICELAND**
18. **IRELAND**
19. **ITALY**
20. **LATVIA**
21. **LIECHTENSTEIN**
22. **LITHUANIA**
23. **LUXEMBOURG**
24. **MACEDONIA**
25. **MALTA**
26. **MOLDOVA**
27. **MONACO**
28. **NETHERLANDS**
29. **NORWAY**
30. **POLAND**
31. **PORTUGAL**
32. **ROMANIA**
33. **RUSSIA** (in Europe)
34. **SAN MARINO** (only a city)
35. **SLOVAKIA**

INDEPENDENT COUNTRIES

36. **SLOVENIA**
37. **SPAIN**
38. **SWEDEN**
39. **SWITZERLAND**
40. **TURKEY** (in Europe)
41. **UKRAINE**
42. **UNITED KINGDOM** (Includes Great Britain)
43. **VATICAN CITY** (obviously a city)
44. **YUGOSLAVIA**

❖ WATERWAYS ❖ POINTS OF INTEREST ❖

ADRIATIC SEA
AEGEAN SEA
ARCTIC CIRCLE
BALTIC SEA
BAY OF BISCAY
BLACK SEA
CASPIAN SEA
ENGLISH CHANNEL
IONIAN SEA
MEDITERRANEAN SEA
NORTH ATLANTIC OCEAN
NORTH SEA
NORWEGIAN SEA
PRIME MERIDIAN
SEA OF AZOV
SKAGGERAK
TYRRHENIAN SEA

BONUS: What is the Prime Meridian?

_____

_____

_____

_____

Europe: Review #1

Use with page forty-seven.

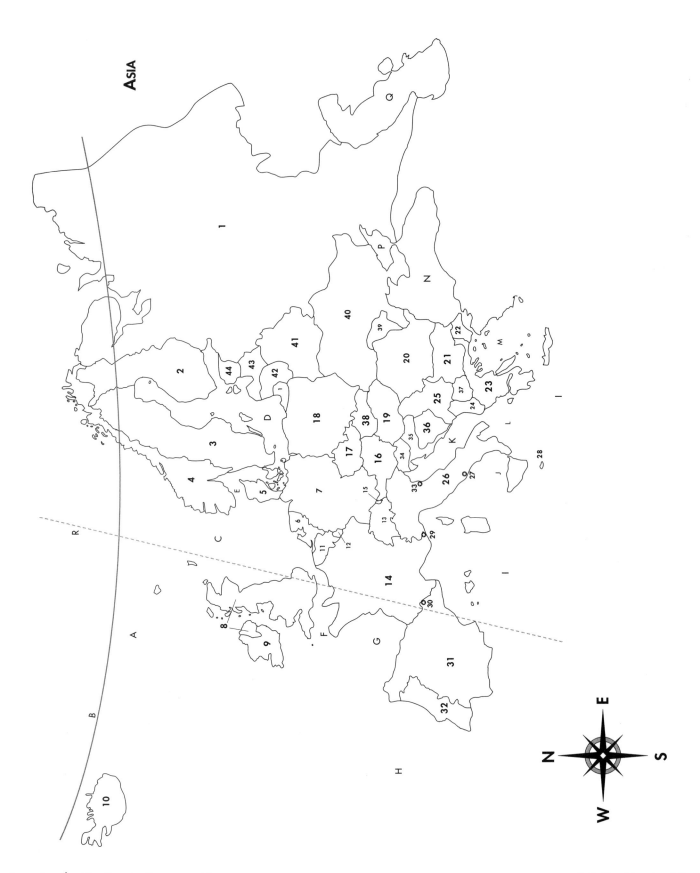

Europe: Review #1

Use with page forty-six.

> Fill in the lines with the correct number or letter using the map provided.
> Note: "O" was not used because it could be mistaken for an island on the map.

INDEPENDENT COUNTRIES

_____	**ALBANIA**
_____	**ANDORRA** (only a city)
_____	**AUSTRIA**
_____	**BELARUS**
_____	**BELGIUM**
_____	**BOSNIA-HERZEGOVINA**
_____	**BULGARIA**
_____	**CROATIA**
_____	**CZECH REPUBLIC**
_____	**DENMARK**
_____	**ESTONIA**
_____	**FINLAND**
_____	**FRANCE**
_____	**GERMANY**
_____	**GREECE**
_____	**HUNGARY**
_____	**ICELAND**
_____	**IRELAND**
_____	**ITALY**
_____	**LATVIA**
_____	**LIECHTENSTEIN**
_____	**LITHUANIA**
_____	**LUXEMBOURG**
_____	**MACEDONIA**
_____	**MALTA**
_____	**MOLDOVA**
_____	**MONACO**
_____	**NETHERLANDS**
_____	**NORWAY**
_____	**POLAND**
_____	**PORTUGAL**
_____	**ROMANIA**
_____	**RUSSIA**
_____	**SAN MARINO** (only a city)
_____	**SLOVAKIA**

INDEPENDENT COUNTRIES

_____	**SLOVENIA**
_____	**SPAIN**
_____	**SWEDEN**
_____	**SWITZERLAND**
_____	**TURKEY** (in Europe)
_____	**UKRAINE**
_____	**UNITED KINGDOM** (Includes Great Britain)
_____	**VATICAN CITY** (obviously a city)
_____	**YUGOSLAVIA**

❖ WATERWAYS ❖ POINTS OF INTEREST ❖

_____	ADRIATIC SEA
_____	AEGEAN SEA
_____	ARCTIC CIRCLE
_____	BALTIC SEA
_____	BAY OF BISCAY
_____	BLACK SEA
_____	CASPIAN SEA
_____	ENGLISH CHANNEL
_____	IONIAN SEA
_____	MEDITERRANEAN SEA
_____	NORTH ATLANTIC OCEAN
_____	NORTH SEA
_____	NORWEGIAN SEA
_____	PRIME MERIDIAN
_____	SEA OF AZOV
_____	SKAGGERAK
_____	TYRRHENIAN SEA

BONUS: Name the 8 European countries that were part of the former Soviet Union.

_____

_____

Europe
Use with page forty-nine.

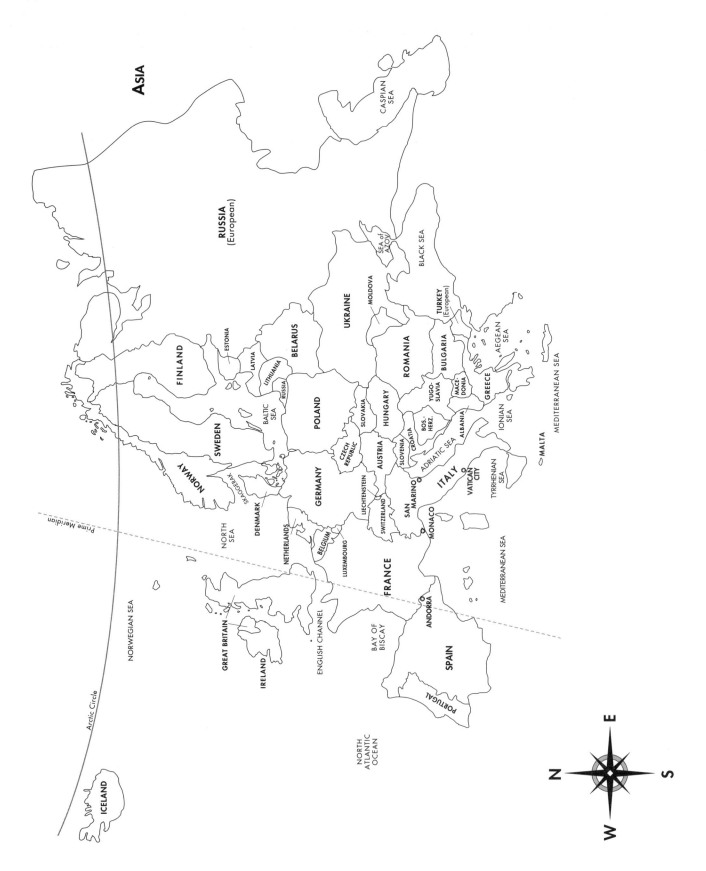

Europe
Use with page forty-eight.

Name _____

Date _____

Trace the outline of Europe and then draw in the countries, etc. Label your map.

ASIA

Europe
Use with page fifty-one.

Name _____

Date _____

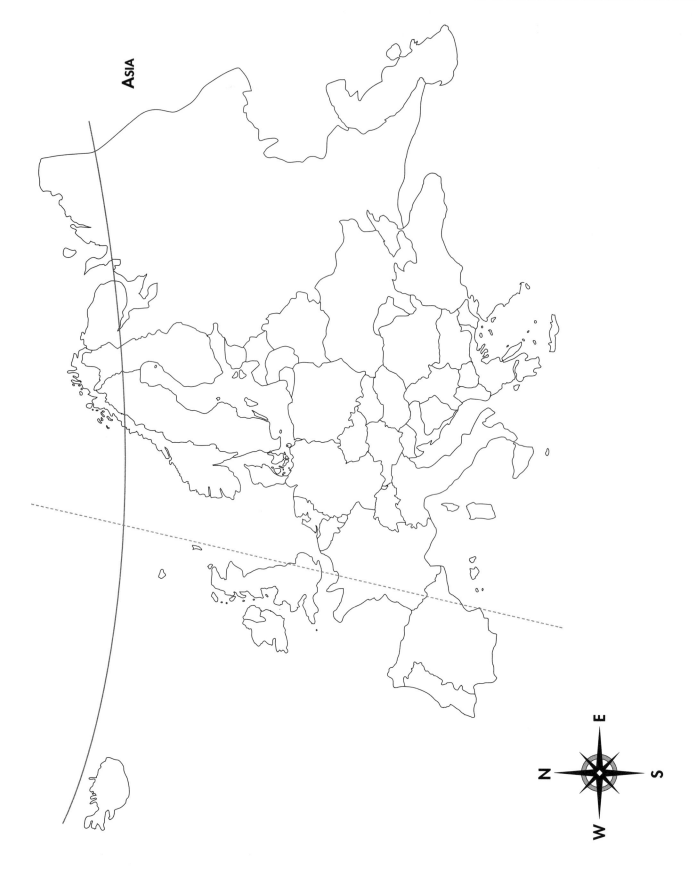

ASIA

Europe
Use with page fifty.

Name _____

Date _____

Fill in the lines with the correct bordering countries and/or waterways using the map provided. The number following the name of each country specifies the number of names you need to write. Note: You might need to complete the map before you begin.

ALBANIA (4) _____

AUSTRIA (8) _____

_____

BELGIUM (6) _____

_____

BULGARIA (6) _____

CZECH REPUBLIC (4) _____

_____

DENMARK (3) _____

FINLAND (4) _____

FRANCE (10) _____

_____

_____

GERMANY (11) _____

_____

_____

GREECE (6) _____

_____

HUNGARY (7) _____

_____

IRELAND (2) _____

ITALY (9) _____

_____

_____

NORWAY (6) _____

_____

PORTUGAL (2) _____

ROMANIA (6) _____

_____

SWEDEN (4) _____

UNITED KINGDOM (4) _____

_____

YUGOSLAVIA (8) _____

_____

Europe: Review #2

Use with page fifty-three.

Name _____

Date _____

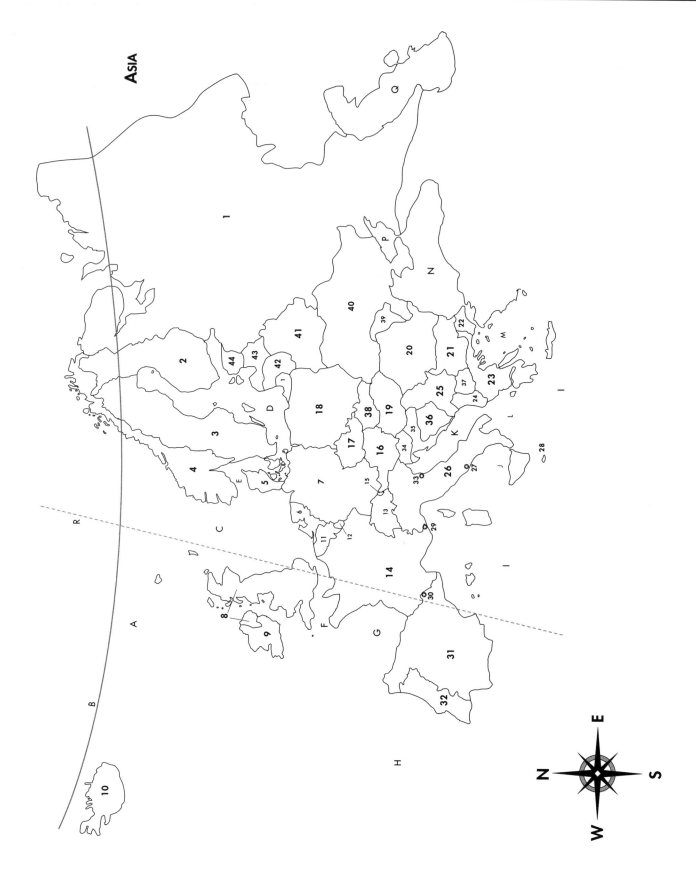

Europe: Review #2

Use with page fifty-two.

Name _____

Date _____

Write the name of the correct answer next to the corresponding number
or letter on the line provided.

INDEPENDENT COUNTRIES

1. _____
2. _____
3. _____
4. _____
5. _____
6. _____
7. _____
8. _____
9. _____
10. _____
11. _____
12. _____
13. _____
14. _____
15. _____
16. _____
17. _____
18. _____
19. _____
20. _____
21. _____
22. _____
23. _____
24. _____
25. _____
26. _____
27. _____
28. _____
29. _____
30. _____
31. _____
32. _____
33. _____
34. _____
35. _____

INDEPENDENT COUNTRIES

36. _____
37. _____
38. _____
39. _____
40. _____
41. _____
42. _____
43. _____
44. _____

❖ Waterways ❖ Points of Interest ❖ ❖ Other Political Units ❖

A. _____
B. _____
C. _____
D. _____
E. _____
F. _____
G. _____
H. _____
I. _____
J. _____
K. _____
L. _____
M. _____
N. _____
P. _____
Q. _____
R. _____

BONUS: Name the 5 countries that used to make up Yugoslavia.

_____

_____

_____

Europe
Word Search
(No space between words.)

Name _____

Date _____

ALBANIA	GERMANY	NORWAY
BALTIC SEA	GREECE	PORTUGAL
BELGIUM	ICELAND	ROMANIA
BULGARIA	IRELAND	SLOVAKIA
CASPIAN SEA	ITALY	SLOVENIA
DENMARK	LIECHTENSTEIN	SPAIN
ENGLAND	LUXEMBOURG	SWITZERLAND
FINLAND	MALTA	TURKEY
FRANCE	NETHERLANDS	YUGOSLAVIA

```
I Z G G W K F A Y H I O H E Q Q L T R R D
T T U R J N L J Y D K C H C P U O X A M W
A I W Q E G I C Y L E N E Y M B U E V A T
L G A E O E A E C E E N A L M I S P I K C
Y U O C L C L T T S D M U A Y U C A K I
P H A G F Z N E H S P L I A F N W M H I D
F W N X X G J E A O N G O G R I D I A K D
R N G D V A R E R N L E P V A K N U A R P
J I F R E L S T B E E E T A A I T L Z M B
A A E N A C U A B S N F A H I K N X A X M
V P Z N I G I I U B R J U Z C R I A I N X
R S D T A N D R T A J O Z Z A E A A B J D
G S L L E N Y A N F G H K K J I I G T L C
D A L V A N D C N J E J N L C K N L L A A
B F O L A N E N U Q O F S L N S H A Y U Q
T L G M A Y K M R D H S P A T L A M M B B
S N R L A T U R K E Y Q A W L N N G T O G
E E E W Y U G O S L A V I A C I X C B A R
G R R I P K S M F K J G R U O B M E X U L
I O C A S P I A N S E A S B N N M K V F U
N S W I T Z E R L A N D W J J O Z X H S L
```

North America
Country Identification

❖ **Please note that the following Independent Countries and Other Political Units (all islands) of North America could not fit onto our maps. You may want to look for them in another resource.**

INDEPENDENT COUNTRIES
ANTIGUA & BARBUDA
BARBADOS
DOMINICA
GRENADA
ST. LUCIA
ST. VINCENT & THE GRENADINES
TRINIDAD & TOBAGO

Other Political Units
Anguilla
Guadeloupe
Martinique
Montserrat
St. Kitts & Nevis
St. Pierre & Miquelon

North America

Use with page fifty-seven.

Name _____

Date _____

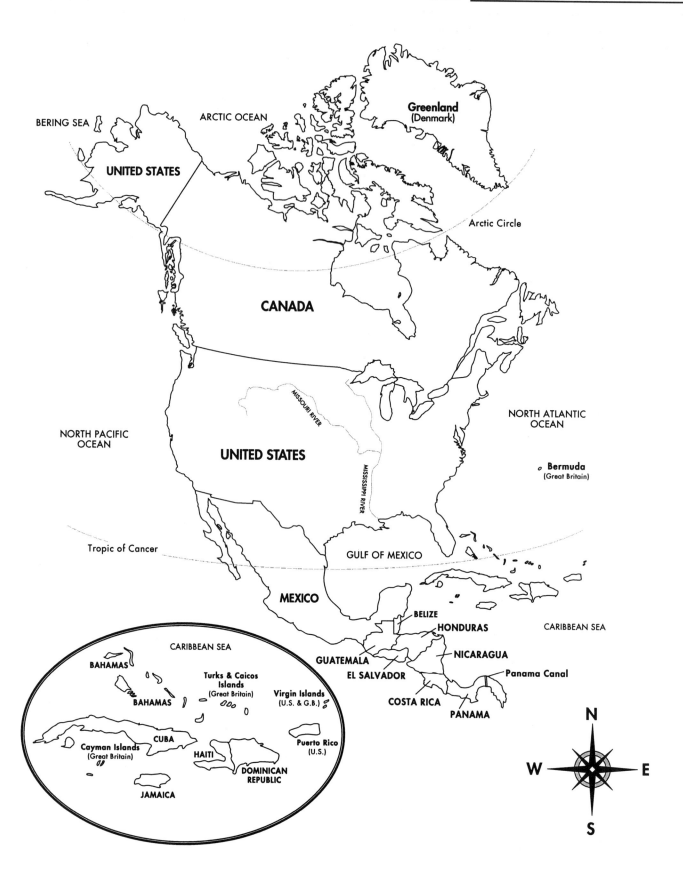

BERING SEA

ARCTIC OCEAN

Greenland
(Denmark)

UNITED STATES

Arctic Circle

CANADA

MISSOURI RIVER

NORTH PACIFIC OCEAN

NORTH ATLANTIC OCEAN

UNITED STATES

Bermuda
(Great Britain)

MISSISSIPPI RIVER

Tropic of Cancer

GULF OF MEXICO

MEXICO

BELIZE

HONDURAS

GUATEMALA

NICARAGUA

CARIBBEAN SEA

EL SALVADOR

Panama Canal

COSTA RICA

PANAMA

CARIBBEAN SEA

BAHAMAS

Turks & Caicos Islands
(Great Britain)

Virgin Islands
(U.S. & G.B.)

BAHAMAS

CUBA

Cayman Islands
(Great Britain)

Puerto Rico
(U.S.)

HAITI

DOMINICAN REPUBLIC

JAMAICA

N
W   E
S

North America

Use with page fifty-six.

Label this map exactly like the map provided. Make sure you print the names the same.

North America

Use with page fifty-nine.

North America

Use with page fifty-eight.

Name _____

Date _____

Fill in the lines with the correct answer in alphabetical order using the map provided.
Note the style of type when choosing the words for the appropriate line.

INDEPENDENT COUNTRIES   MAJOR WATERWAYS   **Other Political Units**   Points of Interest

LAND REGIONS

1. _____
2. _____
3. _____
4. _____
5. _____
6. _____
7. _____
8. _____
9. _____
10. _____
11. _____
12. _____
13. _____
14. _____
15. _____
16. _____
17. _____
18. _____
19. _____
20. _____
31. _____

❖ Points of Interests ❖

_____
_____
_____

Name the two largest islands in North America that are are not part of Canada.

_____
_____

❖ Major Waterways ❖

_____
_____
_____
_____
_____
_____
_____

Name the country that is almost _entirely_ inside the Arctic Circle.

_____

What body of water does the Mississippi River empty into?

_____

Name the oceans that surround North America.

_____
_____
_____

BONUS: Name the state that lies mostly inside the Arctic Circle.

_____

BONUS: Name the 5 Great Lakes.

_____
_____
_____
_____

North America

Use with page sixty-one.

Name _____

Date _____

North America

Name _____

Date _____

Fill in the map provided with the correct country, waterway or point of interest.
Note the style of type when choosing the words for the appropriate label.

INDEPENDENT COUNTRIES   MAJOR WATERWAYS   **Other Political Units**   Points of Interest

INDEPENDENT COUNTRIES

1. **BAHAMAS**
2. **BELIZE**
3. **CANADA**
4. **COSTA RICA**
5. **CUBA**
6. **DOMINICAN REPUBLIC**
7. **EL SALVADOR**
8. **GUATEMALA**
9. **HAITI**
10. **HONDURAS**
11. **JAMAICA**
12. **MEXICO**
13. **NICARAGUA**
14. **PANAMA**
15. **UNITED STATES**

❖ OTHER POLITICAL UNITS ❖

Bermuda (UK/Great Britain)
Cayman Islands (UK/Great Britain)
Greenland (Denmark)
Puerto Rico (United States)
Turks & Caicos Islands (UK/Great Britain)
Virgin Islands (UK/Great Britain)
Virgin Islands (United States)

❖ MAJOR WATERWAYS ❖

ARCTIC OCEAN
BERING SEA
CARIBBEAN SEA
GULF OF MEXICO
MISSISSIPPI RIVER
MISSOURI RIVER
NORTH ATLANTIC OCEAN
NORTH PACIFIC OCEAN

❖ POINTS OF INTEREST ❖

Arctic Circle
Panama Canal
Tropic of Cancer

List the independent countries of North America that are not an island.

_____
_____
_____
_____
_____
_____
_____
_____
_____
_____
_____

BONUS: List the independent countries of North America that are not an island in order of size. Make the largest country number one and the smallest country number ten. (You will probably need another resource book to check each country's square miles.)

_____
_____
_____
_____
_____
_____
_____
_____
_____

North America

Review #1 Use with page sixty-three.

Name _____

Date _____

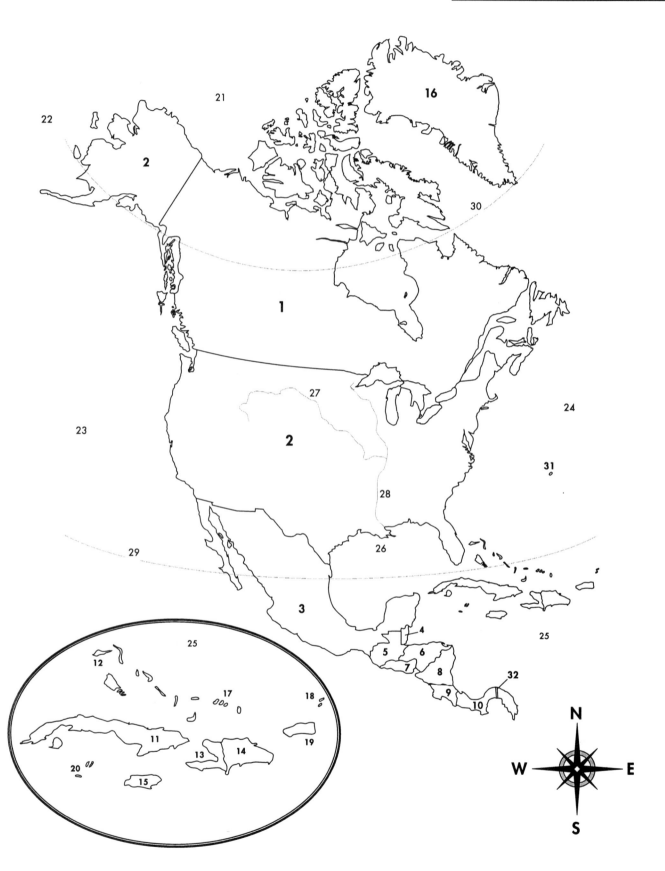

North America

Review #1 Use with page sixty-two.

Fill in the lines with the correct number using the map provided.

LAND REGIONS

_____ BAHAMAS
_____ BELIZE
_____ BERMUDA
_____ CANADA
_____ CAYMAN ISLANDS
_____ COSTA RICA
_____ CUBA
_____ DOMINICAN REPUBLIC
_____ EL SALVADOR
_____ GREENLAND
_____ GUATEMALA
_____ HAITI
_____ HONDURAS
_____ JAMAICA
_____ MEXICO
_____ NICARAGUA
_____ PANAMA
_____ PUERTO RICO
_____ TURKS & CAICOS ISLANDS
_____ UNITED STATES
_____ VIRGIN ISLANDS

List the oceans, seas, gulfs and rivers in alphabetical order.

_____
_____
_____
_____
_____
_____
_____
_____

❖ MAJOR WATERWAYS ❖

_____ ARCTIC OCEAN
_____ BERING SEA
_____ CARIBBEAN SEA
_____ GULF OF MEXICO
_____ MISSISSIPPI RIVER
_____ MISSOURI RIVER
_____ NORTH ATLANTIC OCEAN
_____ NORTH PACIFIC OCEAN

❖ POINTS OF INTEREST ❖

_____ Arctic Circle
_____ Panama Canal
_____ Tropic of Cancer

List the independent countries of North America in <u>reverse</u> alphabetical order.

_____
_____
_____
_____
_____
_____
_____
_____
_____
_____
_____
_____
_____
_____

North America

Use with page sixty-four.

Trace the outline of North America and then draw in the countries, etc. Label your map.

North America

Use with page sixty-seven.

North America

Use with page sixty-six.

Name _____

Date _____

Fill in the lines with the correct bordering countries and/or waterways using the map provided. The number following the name of each country specifies the number of names you need to write. Note: You might need to complete the map before you begin.

BAHAMAS (2) _____

BELIZE (3) _____

BERMUDA (1) _____

CANADA (4) _____
_____

CAYMAN ISLANDS (1) _____

COSTA RICA (4) _____
_____

CUBA (2) _____

DOMINICAN REPUBLIC (2) _____

EL SALVADOR (3) _____

GREENLAND (2) _____

GUATEMALA (6) _____
_____

HAITI (2) _____

HONDURAS (5) _____
_____

JAMAICA (1) _____

MEXICO (6) _____
_____

NICARAGUA (4) _____
_____

PANAMA (4) _____
_____

PUERTO RICO (2) _____

TURKS & CAICOS ISLANDS (2) _____

UNITED STATES (7) _____
_____

VIRGIN ISLANDS (2) _____

North America

Review #2 Use with page sixty-nine.

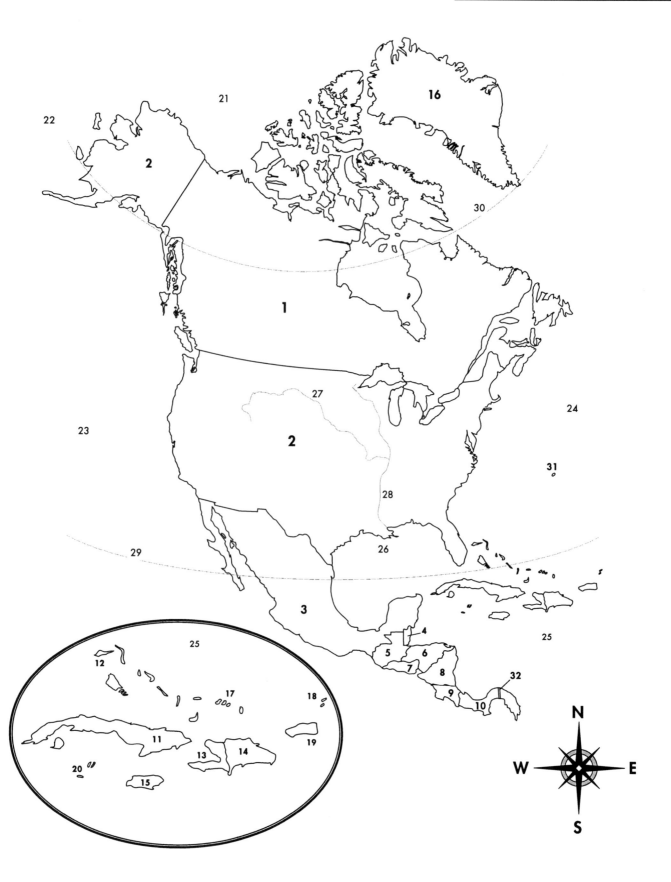

North America

Review #2 Use with page sixty-eight.

Name _____

Date _____

Write the name of the correct answer next to the corresponding number on the line provided.

1. _____
2. _____
3. _____
4. _____
5. _____
6. _____
7. _____
8. _____
9. _____
10. _____
11. _____
12. _____
13. _____
14. _____
15. _____
16. _____
17. _____
18. _____
19. _____
20. _____
21. _____
22. _____
23. _____
24. _____
25. _____
26. _____
27. _____
28. _____
29. _____
30. _____
31. _____
32. _____

List the countries that lie completely or partly between the Equator and the Arctic Circle.

_____
_____
_____
_____
_____

List the independent countries that border the Atlantic Ocean and/or the Caribbean Sea

_____
_____
_____
_____
_____
_____
_____
_____
_____

BONUS: Name the country bordering North America.

_____

BONUS: Name the continent bordering North America.

_____

Name the continent that is to the south of North America.

_____

North America

Word Search
(No space between words.)

Name _____

Date _____

ARCTIC CIRCLE
ARCTIC OCEAN
BAHAMAS
BELIZE
BERING SEA
BERMUDA
CANADA
CARIBBEAN SEA
CAYMAN ISLANDS

COSTA RICA
CUBA
DOMINICAN REPUBLIC
EL SALVADOR
GREENLAND
GUATEMALA
GULF OF MEXICO
HAITI

HONDURAS
JAMAICA
MISSISSIPPI RIVER
NICARAGUA
PACIFIC
PANAMA
PUERTA RICO
UNITED STATES
VIRGIN ISLANDS

```
E D A R C T I C C I R C L E H N E B A P C
G L N S S Y S L C E B M S L D A E L U M A
U A S A A E Q Z E G V N C I D R A E I U Y
L A C A L M Z S X A G D X A M M R S J N M
F C V I L N A I O W B G N U E T S R W I A
O G Y H L V E H L P V A D T A I J J A T N
F X S L P B A E A E C A A R S P C C H E I
M U H K P V U D R B B U I S G B X M C D S
E A C Y B Y M P O G G C I M G F F O G S L
X I N P F Z H C E R O P P Y K E W Q Z T A
I Q D B R U Q P H R N F A X W L R B A N
C E K T A Z A O A I N N I U N W S C K T D
O Y P S I C N C R G E A A C A A J P K E S
U F M T I D I I G L Y T C E A C M V H S J
D P I F U R V W J D A P O I S R I A H V J
M A I R A E R C B H F S H H N G A A H R K
H C A T R X B L Q F U L E B C I N G M F T
J S S L B H G T R K F Z A B U C M I U A T
O O C A R I B B E A N S E A Z D U O R A J
C U H Y L S D N A L S I N I G R I V D E E
A T L A N T I C O C E A N S U D N G V U B
```

South America
Country Identification

South America

Use with page seventy-three.

Name _____

Date _____

CARIBBEAN SEA

NORTH ATLANTIC OCEAN

VENEZUELA

GUYANA (GUIANA)

SURINAME (SURINAM)

French Guiana (France)

COLOMBIA

ECUADOR

Equator

AMAZON RIVER

Galapagos Islands (Ecuador)

Fernando de Noronha (Brazil)

PERU

BRAZIL

SOUTH PACIFIC OCEAN

BOLIVIA

CHILE

PARAGUAY

Trindade Island (Brazil)

Tropic of Capricorn

San Ambrosio Island (Chile)

San Félix Island (Chile)

ARGENTINA

San Fernández Islands (Chile)

URUGUAY

SOUTH ATLANTIC OCEAN

N

W   E

S

Falkland Islands (United Kingdom)

South Georgia Island (Falkland Islands)

Strait of Magellan

Cape Hope

South America

Use with page seventy-two.

Label this map exactly like the map provided. Make sure you print the names the same.

South America

Use with page seventy-five.

Name _____

Date _____

CARIBBEAN SEA

NORTH ATLANTIC OCEAN

VENEZUELA

GUYANA (GUIANA)

SURINAME (SURINAM)

French Guiana (France)

COLOMBIA

Equator

ECUADOR

AMAZON RIVER

Fernando de Noronha (Brazil)

Galapagos Islands (Ecuador)

PERU

BRAZIL

BOLIVIA

SOUTH PACIFIC OCEAN

PARAGUAY

Trindade Island (Brazil)

CHILE

Tropic of Capricorn

San Ambrosio Island (Chile)

San Félix Island (Chile)

ARGENTINA

San Fernández Islands (Chile)

URUGUAY

SOUTH ATLANTIC OCEAN

N

W   E

S

Falkland Islands (United Kingdom)

Strait of Magellan

Cape Hope

South Georgia Island (Falkland Islands)

South America

Use with page seventy-four.

Name _____

Date _____

Fill in the lines with the correct answer in alphabetical order using the map provided.
Note the style of type when choosing the words for the appropriate line.

INDEPENDENT COUNTRIES   MAJOR WATERWAYS   **Other Political Units**   Points of Interest

---

INDEPENDENT COUNTRIES

1. _____
2. _____
3. _____
4. _____
5. _____
6. _____
7. _____
8. _____
9. _____
10. _____
11. _____
12. _____

❖ Other Political Units ❖

_____
_____

❖ Surrounding Islands ❖

_____
_____
_____
_____
_____
_____

❖ Major Waterways ❖

_____
_____
_____
_____
_____

❖ Points of Interests ❖

_____
_____
_____

List the independent countries of South America in order of size with the <u>largest</u> one first.

1. _____
2. _____
3. _____
4. _____
5. _____
6. _____
7. _____
8. _____
9. _____
10. _____
11. _____
12. _____

List the countries of South America that are bordered by the Pacific Ocean.

_____
_____
_____

List the countries of South America that lie <u>completely</u> north of the Equator.

_____
_____
_____

South America

Use with page seventy-seven.

Name _____

Date _____

South America

Name _____

Use with page seventy-six.

Date _____

Fill in the map provided with the correct country, waterway or point of interest.
Note the style of type when choosing the words for the appropriate label.

INDEPENDENT COUNTRIES   MAJOR WATERWAYS   **Other Political Units**   Points of Interest

INDEPENDENT COUNTRIES

1. **ARGENTINA**
2. **BOLIVIA**
3. **BRAZIL**
4. **CHILE**
5. **COLOMBIA**
6. **ECUADOR**
7. **GUYANA**
8. **PARAGUAY**
9. **PERU**
10. **SURINAME**
11. **URUGUAY**
12. **VENEZUELA**

❖ OTHER POLITICAL UNITS ❖
Falkland Islands (UK/Great Britain)
French Guiana (France)

❖ SURROUNDING ISLANDS ❖
Fernando de Noronha (Brazil)
Galapagos (Ecuador)
San Ambrosio Island (Chile)
San Félix Island (Chile)
San Fernández Islands (Chile)
South Georgia Island (Falkland Islands)
Trinidade Island (Brazil)

❖ MAJOR WATERWAYS ❖
AMAZON RIVER
CARIBBEAN SEA
NORTH ATLANTIC OCEAN
NORTH PACIFIC OCEAN
SOUTH ATLANTIC OCEAN
SOUTH PACIFIC OCEAN

❖ POINTS OF INTEREST ❖
Cape Horn
Equator
Strait of Magellan
Tropic of Capricorn

List the countries of South America that are crossed by the Equator.

_____
_____
_____
_____

List the independent countries of South America that in order of size. Make the smallest country number one.

1. _____
2. _____
3. _____
4. _____
5. _____
6. _____
7. _____
8. _____
9. _____
10. _____
11. _____
12. _____

BONUS: What language is mostly spoken in Brazil?

_____

BONUS: What language is mostly spoken in the rest of South America?

_____

South America

Review #1 Use with page seventy-nine.

Name _____

Date _____

South America

Review #1 Use with page seventy-eight.

Name _____

Date _____

Fill in the lines with the correct number using the map provided.

INDEPENDENT COUNTRIES

_____ ARGENTINA
_____ BOLIVIA
_____ BRAZIL
_____ CHILE
_____ COLOMBIA
_____ ECUADOR
_____ GUYANA
_____ PARAGUAY
_____ PERU
_____ SURINAME
_____ URUGUAY
_____ VENEZUELA

❖ **OTHER POLITICAL UNITS** ❖

_____ **Falkland Islands** (UK/GB)
_____ **French Guiana** (France)

❖ **SURROUNDING ISLANDS** ❖

_____ Fernando de Noronha (Brazil)
_____ Galapagos (Ecuador)
_____ San Ambrosio Island (Chile)
_____ San Félix Island (Chile)
_____ San Fernández Islands (Chile)
_____ South Georgia Island (Falkland Islands)
_____ Trinidade Island (Brazil)

❖ **MAJOR WATERWAYS** ❖

_____ AMAZON RIVER
_____ CARIBBEAN SEA
_____ NORTH ATLANTIC OCEAN
_____ NORTH PACIFIC OCEAN
_____ SOUTH ATLANTIC OCEAN
_____ SOUTH PACIFIC OCEAN

❖ **POINTS OF INTEREST** ❖

_____ Cape Horn
_____ Equator
_____ Strait of Magellan
_____ Tropic of Capricorn

List the countries of South America that are crossed by the Tropic of Capricorn.

_____
_____
_____
_____

List the independent countries of South America in <u>reverse</u> alphabetical order.

_____
_____
_____
_____
_____
_____
_____
_____
_____
_____
_____
_____

Name the ocean the Amazon River empties into.

_____

Name the country bordering South America.

_____

South America

Use with page eighty-one.

Name _____

Date _____

CARIBBEAN SEA

NORTH ATLANTIC OCEAN

VENEZUELA

GUYANA (GUIANA)

SURINAME (SURINAM)

French Guiana (France)

COLOMBIA

ECUADOR

Equator

AMAZON RIVER

Fernando de Noronha (Brazil)

Galapagos Islands (Ecuador)

PERU

BRAZIL

SOUTH PACIFIC OCEAN

BOLIVIA

CHILE

PARAGUAY

Trindade Island (Brazil)

Tropic of Capricorn

San Ambrosio Island (Chile)

San Félix Island (Chile)

ARGENTINA

URUGUAY

San Fernández Islands (Chile)

SOUTH ATLANTIC OCEAN

N
W   E
S

Falkland Islands (United Kingdom)

South Georgia Island (Falkland Islands)

Strait of Magellan

Cape Hope

South America

Use with page eighty.

Trace the outline of South America and then draw in the countries, etc. Label your map.

South America

Use with page eighty-three.

Name _____

Date _____

South America

Use with page eighty-two.

Fill in the lines with the correct bordering countries and/or waterways using the map provided.
The number following the name of each country specifies the number of names you need to write.
Note: You might need to complete the map before you begin.

ARGENTINA (6) _____

_____

BOLIVIA (5) _____

_____

BRAZIL (12) _____

_____

_____

CHILE (4) _____

_____

COLOMBIA (6 + 1 in North America) _____

_____

ECUADOR (3) _____

FALKLAND ISLANDS (1) _____

FERNANDO DE NORONHA (1) _____

FRENCH GUIANA (3) _____

GALAPAGOS ISLANDS (1) _____

GUYANA (Guiana) (4) _____

_____

PARAGUAY (3) _____

SAN AMBROSIO ISLAND (1) _____

SAN FÉLIX ISLAND (1) _____

SAN FERNANDEZ ISLAND (1) _____

SOUTH GEORGIA ISLAND (1) _____

SURINAME (Surinam) (4) _____

_____

TRINIDAD ISLAND (1) _____

URUGUAY (3) _____

_____

VENEZUELA (4) _____

South America

Review #2 Use with page eighty-five.

Name _____

Date _____

© Golden Educational Center

South America

Review #2 Use with page eighty-four.

Name _____

Date _____

Write the name of the correct answer next to the corresponding number on the line provided.

1. _____
2. _____
3. _____
4. _____
5. _____
6. _____
7. _____
8. _____
9. _____
10. _____
11. _____
12. _____
13. _____
14. _____
15. _____
16. _____
17. _____
18. _____
19. _____
20. _____
21. _____
22. _____
23. _____
24. _____
25. _____
26. _____
27. _____
28. _____
29. _____
30. _____
31. _____

Name the continent that is to the north of South America.

_____

List the countries that lie completely or partly between the Equator and the Tropic of Capricorn.

_____
_____
_____
_____
_____
_____
_____
_____

List the independent countries that border the Atlantic Ocean and/or the Caribbean Sea

_____
_____
_____
_____
_____
_____

List three points of interest.

_____
_____
_____

BONUS: Name the continent that lies to the south of South America.

_____

South America

Word Search
(No space between words.)

Name _____

Date _____

AMAZON RIVER	CHILE	GUYANA
AMERICA	COLOMBIA	PACIFIC
ARGENTINA	ECUADOR	PERU
ATLANTIC	EQUATOR	SOUTH GEORGIA ISLAND
BOLIVIA	FALKLAND ISLANDS	STRAIT OF MAGELLAN
BRAZIL	FRENCH GUIANA	SURINAME
CAPE HORN	GALAPAGOS ISLANDS	URUGUAY
CARIBBEAN		VENEZUELA

```
P C C B Z X P H L D N M J J K V U H B A F
G N O R R U U T I M P G O L X R O N A M A
G A A L O A M W C A J A A D U A R N W A L
U S L E O D Z E A F I J J G I O I D U Z K
Y E F A B M A I F S D Q U V H T N Q G O L
A D J O P B B U L E M A I E N A W H U N A
N M I J K A I I C D Y L P E L R O N T R N
A B G N M J G R A E O A G S Z Y M N T I D
V U F B M O X O A B C R I T C M H Q U V I
M E I R W V R G S C A A K W A S U U P E S
R O G R H M O E S I I Y P I J G P L X R L
P Y Y U S Q Q U A G S A O A G F G C D O A
U S R K A U R L R X Z L T T C G L X U S N
B S A B A I E O P L N M A L A I O Z R C D
X R H T N U E K O R S T U N A C F J E I S
D I O A Z G Q P U G A J O M D N I I P L Q
W R M E H S A G A R D O C F N S T R C J D
F E N T O R N D S Z L E Z M X X J I E F S
S E U C H I L E C B S O P A K Z L M C M G
V O F R E N C H G U I A N A N Z F L S V A
S W Z Z P N A L L E G A M F O T I A R T S
```

Answer Keys
Country Identification

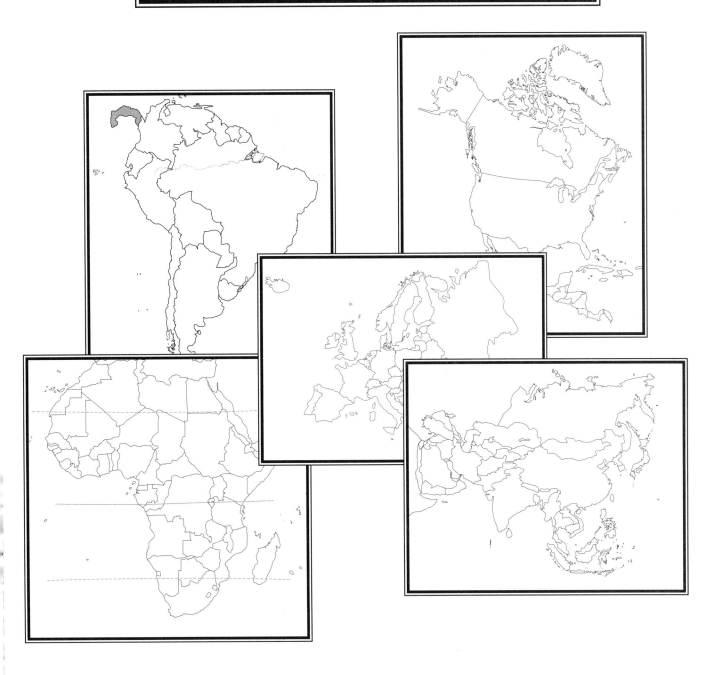

Africa

Answer Key

page 9 – *Teacher Check*

page 11 – *Use list from page 15; (disregard numbering)*

page 15

4	Algeria
31	Angola
19	Benin
47	Botswana
20	Burkina Faso
34	Burundi
28	Cameroon
7	Cape Verde
29	Central African Rep.
22	Chad
42	Comoros
27	Congo
16	Côte d'Ivoire
38	Djibouti
1	Egypt
25	Equatorial Guinea
37	Eritrea
36	Ethiopia
26	Gabon
11	Gambia
17	Ghana
13	Guinea
12	Guinea-Bissau
53	Kenya
49	Lesotho
15	Liberia
2	Libya
43	Madagascar
45	Malawi
8	Mali
6	Mauritania
44	Mauritius
5	Morocco
52	Mozambique
32	Namibia (SW Africa)
9	Niger
21	Nigeria
33	Rwanda
24	São Tomé & Principe
10	Senegal
41	Seychelles
14	Sierra Leone
39	Somalia
51	South Africa
23	Sudan
48	Swaziland
40	Tanzania
18	Togo
3	Tunisia
35	Uganda
30	Democratic Republic of Congo
50	Zambia
46	Zimbabwe

F	Atlantic Ocean
E	Equator
C	Canary Islands (Spain)
N	Gulf of Aden
H	Indian Ocean
B	Madeira Island (Portugal)
A	Mediterranean Sea
J	Red Sea
I	Reunion (France)
L	St. Helena (U.K.)
D	Tropic of Cancer
G	Tropic of Capricorn
K	Walvis Bay (S. Africa)
M	W. Sahara (occ. by Morocco)

page 12 – *Teacher Check*

page 17 – *Teacher Check*

page 19

Algeria: Libya; Mali; Mauritania; Mediterranean Sea; Morocco; Niger; Tunisia; Western Sahara

Angola: Atlantic Ocean; Namibia; Democratic Republic of Congo; Zambia

Benin: Atlantic Ocean; Burkina Faso; Niger; Nigeria; Togo

Botswana: Namibia; South Africa; Zimbabwe

Burundi: Rwanda; Tanzania; Democratic Republic of Congo

Cameroon: Atlantic Ocean; Central African Rep.; Chad; Congo; Equatorial Guinea; Gabon; Nigeria

Chad: Cameroon; Central African Republic; Libya; Niger; Nigeria; Sudan

Congo: Atlantic Ocean; Cameroon; Cenral African Rep.; Gabon; Democratic Republic of Congo

Côte d'Ivoire: Atlantic Ocean; Burkina Faso; Ghana; Guinea; Liberia; Mali

Djibouti: Eritrea; Ethiopia; Gulf of Aden; Somalia

Egypt: Libya; Mediterranean Sea; Red Sea; Sudan

Ethiopia: Djibouti; Eritrea; Kenya; Somalia; Sudan

Gambia: Atlantic Ocean; Senegal

Kenya: Ethiopia; Indian Ocean; Somalia; Sudan; Tanzania; Uganda

Madagascar: Indian Ocean

Niger: Algeria; Benin; Burkina Faso; Chad; Libya; Mali; Nigeria

Nigeria: Atlantic Ocean; Benin; Cameroon; Chad; Niger

Somalia: Djibouti; Ethiopia; Gulf of Aden; Indian Ocean; Kenya

South Africa: Atlantic Ocean; Botswana; Indian Ocean; Lesotho; Mozambique; Namibia; Swaziland; Zimbabwe

Uganda: Kenya; Rwanda; Sudan; Tanzania; Democratic Republic of Congo

page 22 – *See Word Search Keys*

page 21

1. Egypt
2. Libya
3. Tunisia
4. Algeria
5. Morocco
6. Mauritania
7. Cape Verde
8. Mali
9. Niger
10. Senegal
11. Gambia
12. Guinea-Bissau
13. Guinea
14. Sierra Leone
15. Liberia
16. Cote d'Ivoire
17. Ghana
18. Togo
19. Benin
20. Burkina Faso
21. Nigeria
22. Chad
23. Sudan
24. São Tomé & Principe
25. Equatorial Guinea
26. Gabon
27. Congo
28. Cameroon
29. Central African Republic
30. Democratic Republic of Congo
31. Angola
32. Namibia
33. Rwanda
34. Burundi
35. Uganda
36. Ethiopia
37. Eritrea
38. Djibouti
39. Somalia
40. Tanzania
41. Seychelles
42. Comoros
43. Madagascar
44. Mauritius
45. Malawi
46. Zimbabwe
47. Botswana
48. Swaziland
49. Lesotho
50. Zambia
51. South Africa
52. Mozambique
53. Kenya

A. Mediterranean Sea
B. Madeira Island (Portugal)
C. Canary Islands (Spain)
D. Tropic of Cancer
E. Equator
F. Atlantic Ocean
G. Tropic of Capricorn
H. Indian Ocean
I. Reunion (France)
J. Red Sea
K. Walvis Bay (South Africa)
L. St. Helena (U.K.)
M. W. Sahara (occ. by Morocco)
N. Gulf of Aden

Asia
Answer Key

page 25 – *Teacher Check*

page 27 – *Use list from page 31;*
 (disregard numbering)

page 31

18	Afghanistan
16	Armenia
42	Azerbaijan
15	Bahrain
23	Bangladesh
22	Bhutan
51	Brunei
29	Cambodia (Kampuchea)
36	China
4	Cyprus
41	Georgia
20	India
33	Indonesia
17	Iran
8	Iraq
2	Israel
40	Japan
7	Jordan
47	Kazakhstan
37	Korea, North
38	Korea, South
9	Kuwait
45	Kyrgyzstan
27	Laos
3	Lebanon
31	Malaysia
26	Maldives
39	Mongolia
24	Myanmar (Burma)
21	Nepal
12	Oman
19	Pakistan
34	Philippines
14	Qatar
1	Russia (in Asia)
10	Saudi Arabia
32	Singapore
25	Sri Lanka
6	Syria
35	Taiwan
46	Tajikistan
28	Thailand
5	Turkey (in Asia)
43	Turkmenistan
13	United Arab Emirates
44	Uzbekistan
30	Vietnam
11	Yemen
48	Gaza Strip (Egypt)
52	Guam (United States)
50	Hong Kong
49	Macau

G	Arabian Sea
F	Aral Sea
B	Black Sea
I	Bay of Bengal
C	Caspian Sea
K	East China Sea
T	Gulf of Aden
H	Indian Ocean
Q	Kara Sea
R	Laptev Sea

continued on bottom of next column

---

page 28 – *Teacher Check*

page 33 – *Teacher Check*

page 35

Afghanistan: China; Iran; Pakistan; Tajikistan; Turkmenistan; Uzbekistan

Bangladesh: Bay of Bengal; India; Myanmar

Bhutan: China; India

China: Afghanistan; Bhutan; East China Sea; India; Kazakhstan; Kyrgyzstan; Laos; Mongolia; Myanmar (Burma); Nepal; Pakistan; Russia; South China Sea; Tajikistan; Vietnam

India: Arabian Sea; Bangladesh; Bay of Bengal; Bhutan; China; Myanmar (Burma); Nepal; Pakistan

Iran: Armenia; Afghanistan; Arabian Sea; Azerbaijan; Caspian Sea; Iraq; Pakistan; Persian Gulf; Turkey; Turkmenistan

Iraq: Iran; Jordan; Kuwait; Persian Gulf; Saudi Arabia; Syria; Turkey

Israel: Gaza Strip; Egypt; Jordan; Lebanon; Mediterranean Sea; Syria

Japan: North Pacific Ocean; Sea of Japan; Sea of Okhotsk

Kampuchea: Laos; South China Sea; Thailand; Vietnam

Lebanon: Israel; Mediterranean Sea; Syria

Mongolia: China; Russia

Nepal: China; India

Pakistan: Afghanistan; Arabian Sea; China; India; Iran

Russia: Black Sea; Caspian Sea; China; Kara Sea; Kazakhstan; Laptev Sea; Mongolia; N. Korea; Sea of Japan; Sea of Okhotsk;

Saudi Arabia: Black Sea; Iraq; Jordan; Kuwait; Oman; Qatar; Persian Gulf; Red Sea; United Arab Emirates; Yemen

Taiwan: Philippine Sea; East China Sea; South China Sea

Thailand: Bay of Bengal; Cambodia; Laos; Myanmar; South China Sea

Vietnam: China; Cambodia; Laos; South China Sea

page 31 **continued from last column**

A	Mediterranean Sea
M	North Pacific Ocean
D	Persian Gulf
L	Philippine Sea
E	Red Sea
S	Sea of Azov
N	Sea of Japan
P	Sea of Okhotsk
J	South China Sea

---

page 38 – *See Word Search Keys*

page 37

1.	Russia
2.	Israel
3.	Lebanon
4.	Cyprus
5.	Turkey
6.	Syria
7.	Jordan
8.	Iraq
9.	Kuwait
10.	Saudi Arabia
11.	Yemen
12.	Oman
13.	United Arab Emirates
14.	Qatar
15.	Bahrain
16.	Armenia
17.	Iran
18.	Afghanistan
19.	Pakistan
20.	India
21.	Nepal
22.	Bhutan
23.	Bangladesh
24.	Myanmar (Burma)
25.	Sri Lanka
26.	Maldives
27.	Laos
28.	Thailand
29.	Cambodia (Kampuchea)
30.	Vietnam
31.	Malaysia
32.	Singapore
33.	Indonesia
34.	Philippines
35.	Taiwan
36.	China
37.	North Korea
38.	South Korea
39.	Mongolia
40.	Japan
41.	Georgia
42.	Azerbaijan
43.	Turkmenistan
44.	Uzbekistan
45.	Kyrgyzstan
46.	Tajikistan
47.	Kazakhstan
48.	Gaza Strip (Egypt)
49.	Macau
50.	Hong Kong
51.	Brunei
52.	Guam (United States)

A.	Mediterranean Sea
B.	Black Sea
C.	Caspian Sea
D.	Persian Gulf
E.	Red Sea
F.	Aral Sea
G.	Arabian Sea
H.	Indian Ocean
I.	Bay of Bengal
J.	South China Sea
K.	East China Sea
L.	Philippine Sea
M.	North Pacific Ocean
N.	Sea of Japan
P.	Sea of Okhotsk
Q.	Kara Sea
R.	Laptev Sea
S.	Sea of Azov
T.	Gulf of Aden

page 41 – *Teacher Check*

page 43 – Use list from page 47; (disregard numbering)
BONUS: Russia; Turkey; Kazakhstan

page 47

24	Albania
30	Andorra
16	Austria
41	Belarus
11	Belgium
36	Bosnia-Herzegovina
21	Bulgaria
35	Croatia
17	Czech Republic
5	Denmark
44	Estonia
2	Finland
14	France
7	Germany
23	Greece
19	Hungary
10	Iceland
9	Ireland
26	Italy
43	Latvia
15	Liechtenstein
42	Lithuania
12	Luxembourg
37	Macedonia
28	Malta
39	Moldova
29	Monaco
6	Netherlands
4	Norway
18	Poland
32	Portugal
20	Romania
1	Russia (in Europe)
33	San Marino
38	Slovakia
34	Slovenia
31	Spain
3	Sweden
13	Switzerland
22	Turkey (in Europe)
40	Ukraine
8	United Kingdom
27.	Vatican City
25	Yugoslavia

K	Adriatic Sea
M	Aegean Sea
B	Arctic Circle
D	Baltic Sea
G	Bay of Biscay
N	Black Sea
Q	Caspian Sea
F	English Channel
L	Ionian Sea
I	Mediterranean Sea
H	North Atlantic Ocean
C	North Sea
A	Norwegian Sea
R	Prime Meridian
P	Sea of Azov
E	Skaggerak
J	Tyrrhenian Sea

continued on bottom of next column

page 44 – *Teacher Check*

page 49 – *Teacher Check*

page 51

Albania: Adriatic Sea; Ionian Sea; Greece; Macedonia; Yugoslavia

Austria: Czech Republic; Germany; Hungary; Italy; Liechtenstein; Slovakia; Slovenia; Switzerland;

Belgium: English Channel; North Sea; France; Germany; Luxembourg; Netherlands

Bulgaria: Black Sea; Greece; Macedonia; Romania; Turkey; Yugoslavia

Czech Republic: Austria; Germany; Poland; Slovakia

Denmark: Germany; North Sea; Skaggerak

Finland: Baltic Sea; Norway; Russia; Sweden

France: Bay of Biscay; Belgium; English Channel; Germany; Italy; Luxembourg; Mediterranean Sea; Monaco; Spain; Switzerland

Germany: Austria; Baltic Sea; Belgium; Czech Republic; Denmark; France; Luxembourg; Netherlands; North Sea; Poland; Switzerland

Greece: Aegean Sea; Albania; Bulgaria; Ionian Sea; Macedonia; Turkey;

Hungary: Austria; Croatia; Slovakia; Poland; Romania; Slovenia; Ukraine

Ireland: Norwegian Sea; United Kingdom

Italy: Adriatic Sea; Austria; France; Ionian Sea; San Marino; Slovenia; Switzerland; Tyrrhenian Sea; Vatican City

Norway: Finland; North Sea; Norwegian Sea; Russia; Skaggerak; Sweden

Portugal: North Atlantic Ocean; Spain

Romania: Black Sea; Bulgaria; Hungary; Moldova; Ukraine; Yugoslavia

Sweden: Baltic Sea; Finland; Norway; Skaggerak

United Kingdom: English Channel; Ireland; North Sea

Yugoslavia: Adriatic Sea; Albania; Bosnia-Herzegovina; Bulgaria; Croatia; Hungary; Macedonia; Romania

page 47 continued from last column
BONUS:
Belarus; Estonia; Kazakhstan; Latvia; Lithuania; Moldova; Russian Republic; Ukraine

page 54 – *See Word Search Keys*

page 53

1.	Russia (in Europe)
2.	Finland
3.	Sweden
4.	Norway
5.	Denmark
6.	Netherlands
7.	Germany
8.	United Kingdom
9.	Ireland
10.	Iceland
11.	Belgium
12.	Luxembourg
13.	Switzerland
14.	France
15.	Liechtenstein
16.	Austria
17.	Czech Republic
18.	Poland
19.	Hungary
20.	Romania
21.	Bulgaria
22.	Turkey (in Europe)
23.	Greece
24.	Albania
25.	Yugoslavia
26.	Italy
27.	Vatican City
28.	Malta
29.	Monaco
30.	Andorra
31.	Spain
32.	Portugal
33.	San Marino
34.	Slovenia
35.	Croatia
36.	Bosnia-Herzegovina
37.	Macedonia
38.	Slovakia
39.	Moldova
40.	Ukraine
41.	Belarus
42.	Lithuania
43.	Latvia
44.	Estonia

A.	Norwegian Sea
B.	Arctic Circle
C.	North Sea
D.	Baltic Sea
E.	Skaggerak
F.	English Channel
G.	Bay of Biscay
H.	North Atlantic Ocean
I.	Mediterranean Sea
J.	Tyrrhenian Sea
K.	Adriatic Sea
L.	Ionian Sea
M.	Aegean Sea
N.	Black Sea
P.	Sea of Azov
Q.	Caspian Sea
R.	Prime Meridian

BONUS:
Bosnia-Herzegovina; Croatia; Slovenia; Macedonia; Yugoslavia

© Golden Educational Center

North America

Answer Key

page 57 – *Teacher Check*

page 59 – *Use lists from page 63; (disregard numbering)*

Largest Islands: Cuba; Greenland
Country Inside Arctic Circle: Greenland
Mississippi empties into Gulf of Mexico
Sorrounding O.:Arctic; Atlantic; Pacific
BONUS: Alaska
BONUS: Erie; Huron; Michgan;
Ontario; Superior

page 61 Any Order:

Belize
Canada
Costa Rica
El Salvador
Guatemala
Honduras
Mexico
Nicaragua
Panama
United States

In Order of Size: *World Almanac*
1. Canada (3,849,627 sq. mi.)
2. United States (3,618,770 sq. mi.)
3. Mexico (761,604 sq. mi.)
4. Nicaragua (50,193 sq. mi.)
5. Honduras (43,277 sq. mi.)
6. Guatemala (42,042 sq. mi.)
7. Panama (29,762 sq. mi.)
8. Costa Rica (19,652 sq. mi.)
9. Belize (8,867 sq. mi.)
10. El Salvador (8,124 sq. mi.)

page 63

12 Bahamas
4   Belize
31 Bermuda
1   Canada
20 Cayman Islands
9   Costa Rica
11 Cuba
14 Dominican Republic
7   El Salvador
16 Greenland
5   Guatemala
13 Haiti
6   Honduras
15 Jamaica
3   Mexico
8   Nicaragua
10 Panama
19 Puerto Rico
17 Turks & Caicos Islands
2   United States
18 Virgin Islands

Major Waterways
21 Arctic Ocean
22 Bering Sea
25 Caribbean Sea
26 Gulf of Mexico
27 Missouri River
28 Mississippi River
24 North Atlantic Ocean
23 North Pacific Ocean

continued on bottom of the next column

pages 60 & 65 – *Teacher Check*

page 67

Bahamas: Caribbean Sea;
North Atlantic Ocean
Belize: Guatemala; Mexico;
Caribbean Sea
Bermuda: Atlantic Ocean
Canada: Arctic Ocean; North
Atlantic Ocean; North Pacific
Ocean; United States
Cayman Islands: Caribbean Sea
Costa Rica: Caribbean Sea; North
Pacific Ocean; Nicaragua;
Panama
Cuba: Caribbean Sea;
Gulf of Mexico
Dominican Republic: Caribbean Sea;
Haiti
El Salvador: Guatemala; Honduras;
North Pacific Ocean
Greenland: Arctic Ocean;
North Atlantic Ocean
Guatemala: Belize; Caribbean Sea;
El Salvador; Honduras; Mexico
North Pacific Ocean
Haiti: Caribbean Sea; Dominican
Republic
Honduras: Caribbean Sea;
El Salvador; Guatemala;
Nicaragua; North Pacific Ocean
Jamaica: Caribbean Sea
Mexico: Belize; Caribbean Sea:
Guatemala; Gulf of Mexico;
North Pacific Ocean; United States
Nicaragua: Caribbean Sea; Costa
Rica: Honduras; N. Pacific Ocean
Panama: Caribbean Sea: Costa
Rica; N. Pacific Ocean; (S. America
optional)
Puerto Rico: Caribbean Sea;
North Atlantic Ocean
Turks & Caicos Islands: Caribbean
Sea; North Atlantic Ocean
United States: Arctic Ocean;
Bering Sea; Canada; Gulf of
Mexico; Mexico; North Atlantic
Ocean; North Pacific Ocean
Virgin Islands: Caribbean Sea;
North Atlantic Ocean

page 63 continued from last column
Points of Interest
29 Tropic of Cancer
30 Arctic Circle
32 Panama Canal

Reverse ABC Order:
Use the first list shown
under page 61 and reverse
the order.

page 70 – *See Word Search Keys*

page 69
1. Canada
2. United States
3. Mexico
4. Belize
5. Guatemala
6. Honduras
7. El Salvador
8. Nicaragua
9. Costa Rica
10. Panama
11. Cuba
12. Bahamas
13. Haiti
14. Dominican Republic
15. Jamaica
16. Greenland
17. Turks & Caicos Islands
18. Virgin Islands
19. Puerto Rico
20. Cayman Islands
21. Arctic Ocean
22. Bering Sea
23. North Pacific Ocean
24. North Atlantic Ocean
25. Caribbean Sea
26. Gulf of Mexico
27. Missouri River
28. Mississippi River
29. Tropic of Cancer
30. Arctic Circle
31. Bermuda
32. Panama Canal

Continent South of N. America:
South America

Independent Countries Between
Equator & Arctic Circle:
Bahamas
Bermuda
Canada
Greenland
Mexico
United States

Independent Countires Bordering
Atlantic Ocean and/or Caribbean Sea:
Bahamas
Belize
Canada
Costa Rica
Cuba
Dominican Republic
Guatemala
Haiti
Honduras
Jamaica
Nicaragua
Panama
United States

Country South of N. America:
Colombia

South America
Answer Key

page 73 – *Teacher Check*

page 75 – Use list from page 79;
    (disregard numbering)

Other Political Units
    4 Falkland Islands
    1 French Guiana
Surrounding Islands
    19 Fernando de Noronha
    20 Galapagos Islands
    15 San Ambrosio Island
    14 San Félix Island
    16 San Fernández Island
    17 South Georgia Island
    18 Trindade Island
Major Waterways
    27 Amazon River
    21 Caribbean Sea
    22 North Atlantic Ocean
    26 North Pacific Ocean
    23 South Atlantic Ocean
    25 South Pacific Ocean
Points of Interest
    29 Cape Horn
    28 Equator
    24 Strait of Magellan
    30 Tropic of Capricorn

In Order of Size: *World Almanac*
    1. Brazil (3,286,470 sq. mi.)
    2. Argentina (1,065,189 sq. mi.)
    3. Peru (496,222 sq. mi.)
    4. Colombia (439,735 sq. mi.)
    5. Bolivia (424,165 sq. mi.)
    6. Venezuela (352,143 sq. mi.)
    7. Chile (302,779 sq. mi.)
    8. Paraguay (157,047 sq. mi.)
    9. Ecuador (109,483 sq. mi.)
    10. Guyana (83,000 sq. mi.)
    11. Uruguay (68,037 sq. mi.)
    12. Suriname (63,037 sq. mi.)
Bordered by Pacific Ocean
    Chile
    Colombia
    Ecuador
    Peru
Completely North of Equator
    French Guiana
    Guyana
    Suriname
    Venezuela

page 79
    10 Argentina
    31 Bolivia
    3 Brazil
    2 Chile
    12 Colombia
    8 Ecuador
    9 Guyana
    6 Paraguay
    13 Peru
    7 Suriname
    5 Uruguay
    11 Venezuela

Use the list from page 75
for the other items that need
numbers from the map.

continued on bottom of the next column

pages 76 & 81– *Teacher Check*
page 77
Countries Crossed by Equator:
    Brazil
    Colombia
    Ecuador
    Peru

Reverse Order of Size: Use Page 75

    BONUS: Portuguese
    BONUS: Spanish

page 83

Argentina: Bolivia; Brazil: Chile;
Paraguay; South Atlantic Ocean
Uruguay

Bolivia: Argentina; Brazil; Chile;
Paraguay; Peru

Brazil: Argentina; Bolivia; Colombia;
Fr. Guiana; Guyana; N. Atlantic;
Paraguay; Peru; S. Atlantic;
Suriname; Uruguay; Venezuela

Chile: Argentina; Bolivia; Peru;
South Pacific Ocean

Colombia: Brazil; Caribbean Sea;
Ecuador; North Pacific Ocean; Peru;
Venezuela

Ecuador: Colombia;
North Pacific Ocean; Peru

Falkland Islands: South Atlantic Ocean

Fernando de Noronha: N. Atlantic

French Guiana: Brazil;
North Atlantic Ocean; Suriname

Galapagos Islands: N. Pacific Ocean

Guyana: Brazil; North Pacific Ocean;
Suriname; Venezuela

Paraguay: Argentina; Brazil; Bolivia

San Ambrosio Island: S. Pacific Ocean

San Félix Island: South Pacific Ocean

San Fernández island: South Pacific

South Georgia Island: South Atlantic

Suriname: Brazil; Fr. Guiana; Guyana;
North Atlantic Ocean

Trinidade Island: South Atlantic Ocean

Uruguay: Argentina; Brazil;
South Atlantic Ocean

Venezuela: Brazil; Caribbean Sea;
Colombia; Guyana

page 79 continued from last column
    Argentina
    Brazil
    Chile
    Paraguay

Use the alphabetical list
from page 79 and reverse it.

Amazon Empties Into: Atlantic Ocean

Country Bordering S. America: Panama

page 86 – *See Word Search Keys*
page 85
    1. French Guiana
    2. Chile
    3. Brazil
    4. Falkland Islands
    5. Uruguay
    6. Paraguay
    7. Suriname (Surinam)
    8. Ecuador
    9. Guyana
    10. Argentina
    11. Venezuela
    12. Colombia
    13. Peru
    14. San Félix Island
    15. San Ambrosio Island
    16. San Fernández Island
    17. South Georgia Island
    18. Trindade Island
    19. Fernando de Noronha
    20. Galapagos Islands
    21. Caribbean Sea
    22. North Atlantic Ocean
    23. South Atlantic Ocean
    24. Strait of Magellan
    25. South Pacific Ocean
    26. North Pacific Ocean
    27. Amazon River
    28. Equator
    29. Cape Horn
    30. Tropic of Capricorn
    31. Bolivia

Continent to the north: North America

Countries that lie between
Equator and Tropic of Capricorn:
    Argentina
    Bolivia
    Brazil
    Chile
    Colombia
    Ecuador
    Paraguay
    Peru

Countries bordering Atlantic
Ocean and/or Caribbean Sea:
    Argentina
    Brazil
    Colombia
    Guyana
    Suriname
    Uruguay
    Venezuela

Three Points of Interest:
    Cape Hope
    Equator
    Tropic of Capricorn

    BONUS: Antarctica

Word Search

Answer Keys

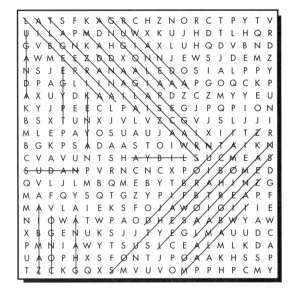

AFRICA

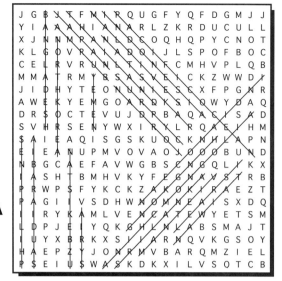

ASIA

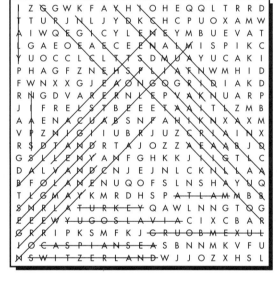

EUROPE

NORTH AMERICA

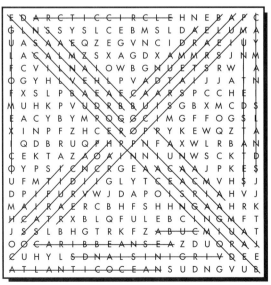

SOUTH AMERICA

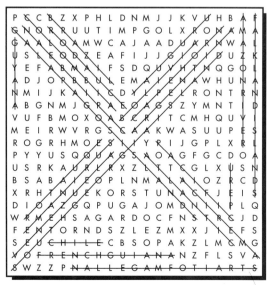

NOTES & DOODLES